I0799446

AMERICAN PT BOATS VOLUME TWO

AMERICAN PT BOATS IN WORLD WAR II

Volume Two

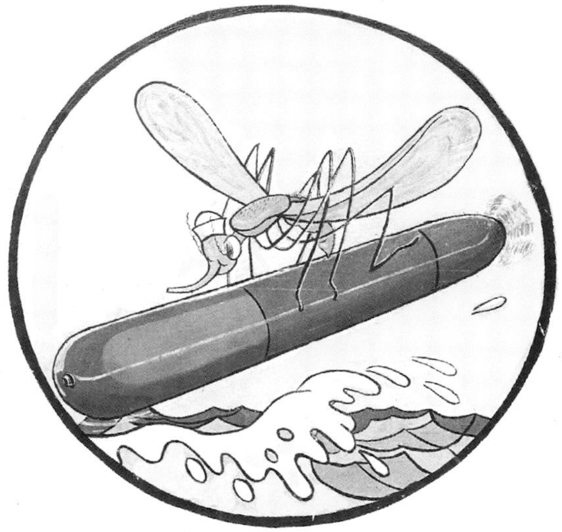

Victor Chun

Schiffer Military History
Atglen, PA

Dedication

To my wonderful wife, Susan, who has taken great care of me for more than 45 years, and my lovely daughter, Vicky, who has been a great help with this volume.

I would also like to dedicate this book to my late parents, Jinsie and Hong Cha, who instilled in me the discipline, perseverance and faith in God.

Book Design by Ian Robertson.

Copyright © 2011 by Victor Chun.
Library of Congress Control Number: 2011915309

All rights reserved. No part of this work may be reproduced or used in any forms or by any means – graphic, electronic or mechanical, including photocopying or information storage and retrieval systems – without written permission from the copyright holder.

Printed in China.
ISBN: 978-0-7643-3948-6

We are interested in hearing from authors with book ideas on related topics.

Published by Schiffer Publishing Ltd.
4880 Lower Valley Road
Atglen, PA 19310
Phone: (610) 593-1777
FAX: (610) 593-2002
E-mail: Info@schifferbooks.com.
Visit our web site at: www.schifferbooks.com
Please write for a free catalog.
This book may be purchased from the publisher.
Please include $5.00 postage.
Try your bookstore first.

In Europe, Schiffer books are distributed by:
Bushwood Books
6 Marksbury Avenue
Kew Gardens
Surrey TW9 4JF, England
Phone: 44 (0) 20 8392-8585
FAX: 44 (0) 20 8392-9876
E-mail: Info@bushwoodbooks.co.uk.
Visit our website at: www.bushwoodbooks.co.uk

Contents

Acknowledgments

This second volume would not have been possible without the help and support of the following people and organizations.

• Robert Biondi and Ian Robertson from Schiffer Publishing, who have been a great support since Volume I. Thank you for answering my numerous questions and allowing for this volume to be published.

• The PT Boat Museum's website "Message Board". I enjoyed reading and corresponding with other PT boat experts.

• Richard J. Washichek, the best graphic artist I have had the privilege to work with. His unique isometric drawings grace many pages of this book.

• Al Ross, who rescued the only drawing of PT 809 from oblivion.

• Frank J. Andruss, his private PT Boat Museum enables the public to view rare photos from his vast collection.

• Alyce N. Guthrie, Executive Vice President and Curator of the PT Boat Museum located in Germantown, TN. My research on PT boats would not have been possible without her and her daughter, Allyson G. Bethune's (Assistant to the Executive Vice President) professionalism and expertise.

• William Smallahaw, who provided me with Irwin Chase's patent for the Elcoplane. Without his help, the function of the louvers on the sides of the Elco boat would have been a guess at best.

• Kathy Brawn for her editing talent

• Ryan Baker, Frank Boyd, Alex Chun, Cathy Costello, Jeremiah Hergott and Dick Washichek for their endless patience and guidance working with me on the digital content of this book.

• Donald Brown, Steve Nugent, and Nathaniel Smith (their fathers served as PT boat skippers), who shared their respective fathers' photos.

• The U. S. Navy, the national archives, the PT Boat Museum, and the many people who provided me with the photos that are published in this book.

• Victoria Chun, my daughter, who helped me with this transcript and accompanied me on my research trip. Her typing speed is beyond my wildest imagination.

Foreword

Never have I encountered a PT boat veteran who called himself a hero. All the men I've known through PT boats, Inc. are humble. They always say they were just doing their job, the country needed them and they went. They went without question paying heavy prices along the four-year journey that was WWII.

I grew up with PT boats. On family vacations when I was a child, I remember my father stopping in so many towns, cities and farms to say hello or look for a PT veteran. Then the period of college, marriage, children and business interrupted my association with the organization. In 1982 it picked back up when I was asked to write some biographies to go in a 40-year history of PTs. Those writings grew into a full time job. It's a job that is so much more than a job. It sounds trite to say that, but it is so true. I am privileged to work for a remarkable organization of remarkable men and their families.

To say knowing, working for, and being with these men is an honor is an understatement of the greatest degree. My years in the PT boat veterans' realm and the success of their reunions, museum and archives could not be improved upon. Had I taken any other job, I wouldn't have ever known important men of such high caliber, nor what a role they played in WWII.

Generally speaking, if you describe something as "unique" in journalism class, the professor will chastise you. But I would use that word to describe PT boat men. During the war, the media latched onto the PT boat and the PT sailors and officers because the country needed articles and film that were uplifting. PT men were seen as dashing riders astride their charging steeds. Their deeds were widely published, so on the Home Front they were highly regarded. Even so, most of the actions and operations were done quietly and unknowingly. Through stealth, conviction and perseverance they met enemies head-on. PTs challenged Axis navies in David and Goliath mode, putting the men at great risk. Yet, I've never heard them complain. In fact, many that I've known said they would do it all again. Many did go to Korea and a few to Vietnam. Through all the very close contact with the Axis, amid the carnage that comes with war and skirting death or coming head-to-head with it on their patrols, when they talk about WWII today, they do not complain about horrible conditions, long absences from home, or the great danger that so often slapped them in the face.

PTs were more frequently in contact and at close range with the enemy than any other surface vessels. They faced a world-wide battle under-supplied and ill-equipped. Yet they never received hazardous duty pay.

In my years as the board-appointed executive vice president, every veteran who has touched my life has brought me another step closer to understanding what a watershed event the war was. I believe with all my being that we Americans will forever be affected by these men riding those beautiful little expendable wooden boats. It is my honor to know the men who rode the boats, manned the tenders, and worked ashore in the PT bases. It is my privilege to help in some small way to keep their stories and history alive.

PT men may not have received their due from the Navy, the boats may not have displaced the amounts a battleship did, but I stand in awe of them.

How could I not?

Alyce N. Guthrie
Executive Vice President WWII PT Boat Museum and Archives

Introduction

This volume has enabled me to present the PT boats' service and contributions in World War II. Beyond the bravery and sacrifices of the PT boat crews and support groups throughout the war, there were three significant historical moments for PT boats. First, to defend the Philippines against a Japanese invasion six PT boats of Squadron 3, under the command of Lt. Bulkeley, were the only Navy to engage the enemy. Although all six boats were lost, their heroic actions bought the U. S. time to rebuild the new Navy. Second, during the early U. S. invasion of Guadalcanal, the U. S. warships were forced to make a tactical retreat due to the vastly superior Japanese forces. The PT boat squadrons were the only U. S. Navy forces that stayed behind to combat the Japanese destroyers shelling the beleaguered Marines on the island. Although vastly outnumbered and outgunned, the PT boats' guerilla type attacks at night so unnerved the Japanese that the bombardment of Henderson Field stopped. For a while, the survival of the Marines and the entire campaign was in doubt. Third, at the Battle of the Surigao Strait, PT boats made first contact with the Japanese fleet as they entered the southern entrance of the strait. Several torpedo hits were observed. However, the most important part of their mission was to report the position of Japanese ships as they moved up the strait. With such intelligence, the U. S. capitol ships were able to position themselves to cross the Japanese ships' "T" and destroy them.

In addition, like Volume I, this volume is also a pictorial presentation. Many modelers have contacted me through the years for pictures and drawings in order to provide the most authentic model. Therefore, I have specifically added drawings and pictures of different types and makes of PT boats from the Pacific to the European Theater of Operation.

Victor K. Chun

For more information on the mentioned actions read *At Close Quarters* by Robert J. Bulkeley

1

Pearl Harbor and the Philippines

First Action at Pearl Harbor

It was December 7, 1941, and on this peaceful Sunday morning, waves of Japanese torpedo planes, escorted by fighters, roared in from the north at low level heading straight for the battleships moored in pairs at "Battleship Row. " At the Submarine base, six of the Squadron 1 PT boats (Elco 77 footers) were berthed in three nests of two each. The crews were just finishing their breakfast on board a submarine barge serving as a tender for the squadron. The Duty Officer, Ensign N. E. Ball, standing on the end of the barge, first spotted the insignia of the "Rising Sun" on the low flying planes and immediately gave the order to "man the guns!" The crews immediately returned to their boats, and Machinists Mates dashed into the engine room to start the air compressor which provided air for the two twin .50 caliber machine gun turrets. All personnel, regardless of rank, either manned the guns or started breaking out and belting more ammunition. They opened fire on the Japanese torpedo planes as they flew over the PT boats on their runs against the battleships. When the planes were flying in a straight line away from the PT boats, gunners on PT23 were able to maintain a steady stream of tracers onto the underside of the planes. One plane burst into flames and crashed near Kuahua Island. The tracer streams from other PT boat guns were also passed onto a second torpedo plane, which was seen to fall in flames in the vicinity of Halawa.

It was later confirmed that the PT boats were the first vessels that opened fire on the enemy and the first to extract casualties from them.

During a lull in the attack, the PT boats got underway and scattered around the harbor so that a hit on one would not endanger them all. After the raid they were sent to the harbor entrance to patrol for submarines. About six miles southwest of the #1 channel buoy a submarine periscope was sighted. PT boats did not carry depth charges at that time; therefore, a destroyer was contacted and led to the area. Several depth charges were dropped; however, there was no immediate evidence that the submarine sank. It wasn't until 20 years later that the remains of the Japanese mini-sub were found at the ocean bottom near the mouth of Pearl Harbor. The bombing of Pearl Harbor was the first day in the long history of PT boats' participation in World War II.

PT261 (Huckins) Ron 26 entering dry dock cradle at Pearl Harbor. It was placed in service June 30, 1943, and assigned to the Hawaiian Sea Frontier, but saw no enemy action. *Courtesy of L. W. Confer*

The PT261 is inside the dry dock for repair. *Courtesy of L. W. Confer*

This is a rare picture of a Huckins PT262 Ron 26 around Pearl Harbor. Only 19 Huckins were built during WWII. *Courtesy of L. W. Confer*

This is PT262 loading a torpedo at Pearl Harbor. *Courtesy of L. W. Confer*

PT258 is underway in the vicinity of the Hawaiian Islands. *Courtesy of L. W. Confer*

MTB Ron 26. Fred Lundy firing a practice torpedo at a destroyer off of Pearl Harbor.
Courtesy of the PT Boat Museum

Ron 1 PT boat underway next to tender *Hammondsport* at Pearl Harbor.
Courtesy of the U. S. Navy

Lt. Commander Earl S. Caldwell was the commander of Ron 1 and 2.
Courtesy of the PT Boat Museum

The Defense of the Philippines

In the Philippines, Motor Torpedo Squadron 3 consisted of six Elco 77 footers and was based at the Cavite Navy Yard under the command of Lt. Bulkeley. In addition to their standard guns, these boats were equipped with a pair of .30 caliber Lewis machine guns on the forward deck. They went into action on 10 December when the Japanese made their first air raid in the Manila Bay area. Several bombers dove on the PT boats while they were underway in Manila Bay. The boats maneuvered expertly and were unharmed. They brought down three enemy planes during this brief encounter.

The raid destroyed almost the entire Navy Yard, in which all the PT boats' parts, gasoline, and equipment were stored. This loss caused extreme hardship for the PT boat crews throughout the defense of the Philippines. In anticipation of more air raids, Squadron 3 moved to Sisiman Bay, at the southern tip of the Bataan Peninsula, where they took up the duty of patrolling the Bataan coast. On 24 December PT33 went aground on a coral reef. After all attempts to move her failed, she was set afire to prevent her from falling into enemy hands. This was the first loss suffered by the squadron.

On the night of January 20, 1941, PT34, commanded by Lt. Bulkeley, snuck into Binanga Bay alone to attack enemy ships reported lying off shore. As the boat was about five hundred yards inside the bay, a two masted 5000 ton armed freighter loomed ahead. The freighter opened fire, which brought the shore battery into action too. PT34 fired two torpedoes. One torpedo got stuck in the tube, but the other ran straight and smashed into the hull of the freighter. Bulkeley spun his boat in a tight arc, swerving and weaving at top speed, heading for the open sea. The sinking of the Japanese freighter was confirmed by Army observers.

As the battle of the Philippines went on, PT boats were rapidly deteriorating due to the lack of spare parts. During a routine patrol along the eastern shore of Subic Bay, the strainers of both wing engines of PT31 were clogged because the gasoline was sabotaged with wax. With two engines stopped the boat drifted on to a reef. Repeated attempts to back off failed, and with shore guns firing at them, the crew abandoned ship. Now only four boats remained.

PT42 of Ron 1 at Pearl Harbor, April 1942.
Courtesy of National Archives

Since the fall of Corregidor was inevitable, General MacArthur was ordered to break through the Japanese blockade and proceed to Australia. With the reply of "We go with the fall of the moon; We go during the Ides of March," the General and his party of twenty-one left Corregidor in the gathering dusk of 11 March on board four PT boats for Mindanao, the first leg of their journey to Australia. They slipped out of Manila Bay headed for Tagauayan.

The sea was rough, and with sheets of water splashing over the bow to obstruct vision, the boats soon became separated. Later they rendezvoused at Tagauayan and PT32 was forced to stay there because of engine trouble. Under very bad weather with frequent rain squalls, the remaining three boats continued their journey toward Cagayan, on Mindanao. They reached their destination safely. They had come through 560 miles of Japanese controlled water without being spotted by the patrolling enemy destroyers.

This was due mostly to the PT boats' high speed and low profile. This evacuation will always be remembered as one of the great feats in the annals of the United States Navy. A lesser known exploit of the PT boats was the evacuation of the Philippines' President Manuel Quezon and his family on board PT41 from Dumaguete to Oroquieta. During the 60 mile trip, a heavy wave jolted the torpedo half way out of the tube with its propeller spinning at high speed. Fortunately, the torpedo man quickly fired the torpedo manually before it detonated. They reached their destination at 6 o'clock in the morning. After PT34 was repaired at Cebu she resumed her patrol duty with PT41.

On the night of 8 April, they spotted a heavily armed Japanese light cruiser just 2 miles off the tip of Cebu. PT41 led the way and fired two torpedoes which straddled the cruiser's bow and stern. Increasing speed to get closer, she fired her remaining two torpedoes, which ran true but no explosion was seen. Meanwhile, PT34 started her run and discharged two torpedoes at 500 yards. Both missed astern. Having seen the white trails of the torpedoes, the cruiser's searchlight swept the night and held PT34 in the beam. Heading for the PT boat, salvos from the cruiser's main battery blew away the mast of PT34 and wounded several crewmen. When the pursuing cruiser got within 300 yards PT34 fired her last torpedoes, then retired by zigzagging violently at maximum speed. As the cruiser turned to cut off the escaping PT boat, two spouts of water were seen at the cruiser's water line. All the searchlights went out and guns suddenly stopped firing. Japanese records captured after the war indicated that the cruiser took one hit, but the torpedo failed to explode.

On her way to Cebu to get medical aid for her crew, PT34 was attacked by four enemy planes while in a narrow channel. The boat was riddled with bullets and the engine room flooded. Skipper Lt. Kelly managed to beach the boat, but the enemy plane returned later and set her on fire. On April 12, 1941, with PT35 still under repair, it was destroyed in the slipway at Cebu as the Japanese entered the city. PT41 was taken over by the Army to be used as a patrol boat and was hauled by truck to Lake Lanao. With the Japanese forces closing in, she was destroyed on the mountain road to the lake.

Even with the loss of all boats of Squadron 3, their sacrifice showed the U. S. Navy the formidable value of the swift PT boat. Based on their actual combat experience, the Navy was able to improve the later PT boats and developed new tactics that eventually inflicted devastating damage to the enemy in years to come.

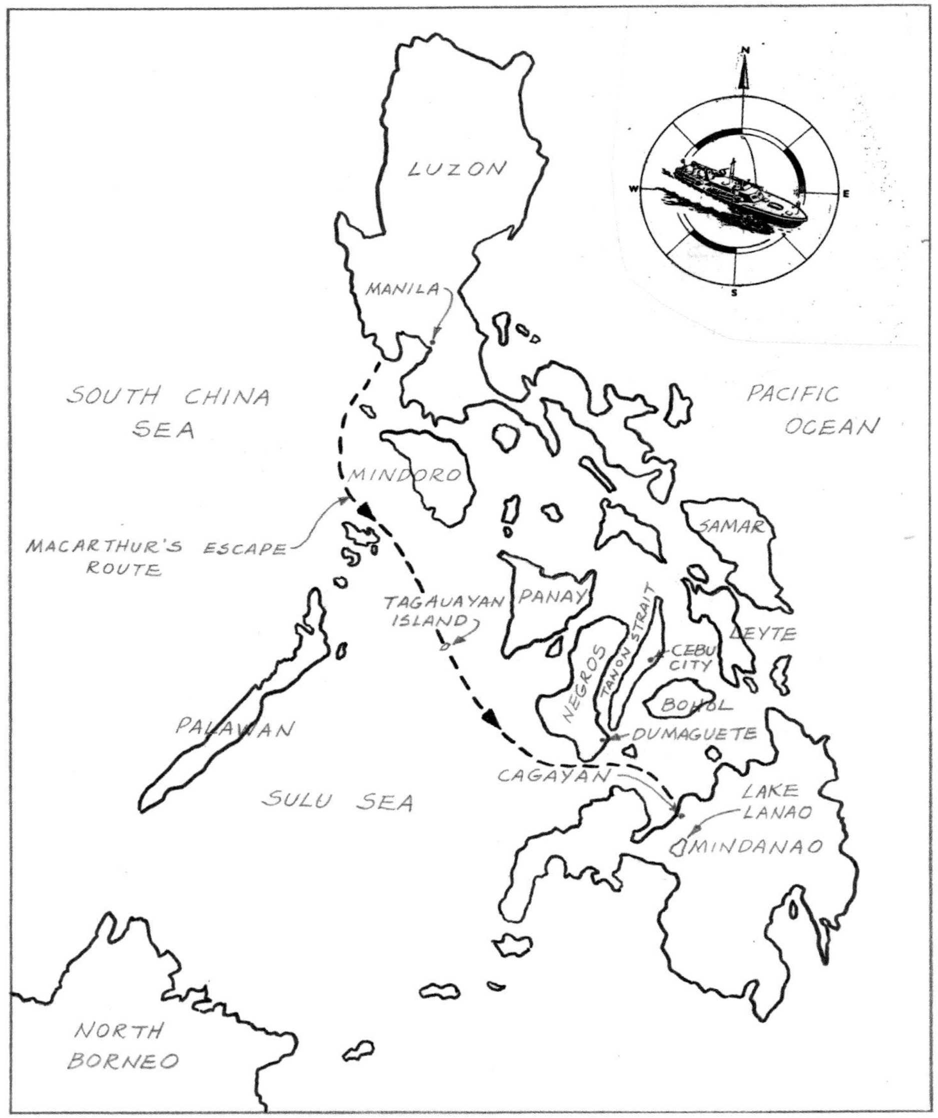

Map of the Philippines

This is a photo of Rear Admiral Frances Rockwell in the Manila area "Headquarter. " He was in command of all naval forces, including PT boat Squadron 3. *Photo courtesy of Rockwell family*

Manila Harbour, Philippines, November 1941. Ron 3 boats steam into the port as seen from the HMCS *Prince Robert* merchant ship, which laid over en route from Canada to Hong Kong. *Courtesy of Don S. Montgomery and the Canadian Public Archives*

Ron 3, PT 41, on board transport bound for the Philipines in 1941. *Courtesy of PT Boat Museum*

The only photograph of Lt. Edward G. Delong's PT31 on board teh tanker *Guadalupe* en route to the Philippines, August 1941. Note the 30 cal. Lewis marchine gun (covered) mounted forward of the chart house. *Courtesy of Mark and James Culp*

Pictured is Edward G. Delong in his United States Naval Academy class (1937) photos. He was the skipper of PT31, Ron 3, which was lost January 18, 1942. After he had lost PT31, he was given command of the USS *Trabajador*, which was lost off Corregidor to Japanese artillery. Officer Delong was eventually captured when he and a fellow officer attempted to escape from Mindano Island via a native boat. They were executed July 2, 1942. He was awarded the Silver Star and the Navy Cross. *Courtesy of Gene K. and Mark Culp*

Ron 3 aboard the SS *Guadalupe* on the way to the Philippines. *Courtesy of Michael*

Right: Lt. Robert B. Kelly, executive officer of the famed Squadron 3, awarded the Navy Cross for sinking a Japanese light cruiser as commander of PT43 off Cebu Island on the nights of April 8 and 9, 1942. This picture was taken after he was evacuated from the Philippines on board a PT boat. *Courtesy of the National Archives*

This is PT34 on a tanker's well deck en route to the Philippines in 1941. *Courtesy of the National Archives*

Lt. Commander John D. Bulkeley, commander of Ron 3 in the Philippines. *Courtesy of the National Archives*

An extremely rare picture of PT 32 in the Philippines. This picture was taken by James D. Culp of PT 32, who was the gunners mate on PT 31. Note the Lewis guns mounted on board. *Courtesy of Mark Culp*

The Brief Encounter at Midway

Late in May 1942, ten Elco 77 foot boats of Squadron 1 at Pearl Harbor proceeded under their power for Midway to reinforce the island for the imminent attack by the Japanese Task Force. On June 4, 1942, shortly after their arrival, 108 Japanese dive bombers and Zero fighters from four carriers struck Midway. The air raid alarm gave the PT boats time to get underway and deeply into combat V formation in the lagoon. As the bombers flew over the bay after dropping their bombs, all the PT boats opened fire on them. Several escort fighters started to dive toward the speedy little boats, but swerved off as a hail of defensive fire came too close. One low flying Zero, however, ran into the deadly cone of machine gun tracers and blew up in a blinding flash into a thousand pieces, which fluttered down, making numerous white splashes in the blue sea.

Just before sunset on June 10, 1942, after the conclusion of the Battle of Midway, two PT boats left the coast embarked on a unique burying mission. Each boat bore two wooden coffins adorned with the insignia of the rising sun. To be buried were four Japanese naval aviators who had crashed on Midway. As the sun settled gradually down the vast expanse of the ocean, dispersing its majestic rays across the Pacific sky, the PT boats moved slowly out to deep water with their flags at half mast. After the services were read by a chaplain three volleys were fired by the Marines, and the coffins were lowered gently overboard. When men die bravely for their country, even though their cause may be wrong, they sometimes are buried with full military honors when the conditions of war permit it.

The Aleutians and the Merciless Weather

The Japanese occupied Attu and Kiska, at the western tip of the Aleutians chain, since June 6, 1942. No counter attack was mounted by the United States until August of that year because of the urgent preparation for the campaign in the Solomons. With a string of 69 islands, innumerable passes and channels in the Aleutians, PT boats were thought to be the ideal vessels used in neutralizing enemy shipping and to support landing under the ever present Aleutian fog.

On July, 1942, four Elco 77 foot type PT boats left Pearl Harbor on board SS *Irvin MacDowell* for Seattle. After overhaul and installation of 20 mm guns, the four boats (PTs 22, 24, 27 and 28) sailed north under their own power and arrived at Dutch Harbor, southwest of the Alaska Peninsula, in September. They found the rough seas and swift currents running

PT42 first saw action at Pearl Harbor on December 7, 1941, and saw action again at the Battle of Midway. *Photo courtesy of U. S. Navy*

along the jagged shorelines extremely hazardous, as the Aleutian weather is known to be the worst in the world. The interaction of the cold wind from Siberia and the arm air from the Pacific causes high velocity wind and dense fog.

To aid navigation in the adverse weather condition, a radar was installed on one PT boat. Still, she went aground on submerged rocks dotted around the islands. After being pulled free and repaired, she joined the other PT boats to set up base at Adak, only 200 miles east of Kiska. They then carried out reconnaissance, mine laying and supply missions. When winter approached, heavy layers of frost constantly formed on the inside of the boat's bulkheads. Lashed by hail and snow when underway, the boats were always covered with 4 inch thick ice from bow to stern; oil congealed in engines, machine guns froze, and torpedo tubes refused to function. The four PT boats were not faring well in the Aleutians; two collided in a squall and suffered some damage, and one went aground and was smashed to pieces by the heavy surf. Another one was dropped from a crane while being loaded aboard a Liberty ship.

With only two PT boats left and the invasion of Attu coming up, Squadron 13, the first Higgins boat squadron, was sent to Adak from Seattle. During the landing on the bleak and treeless Attu in May 1943, the PT boats were used for patrolling to keep the enemy from sending reinforcements. However, no contact was made. After the capture of Attu, the PT boats were used mostly for escorting duty and transportation of high ranking officers.

In September of that year, Squadron 13 was joined by Squadron 16 for the invasion of the heavily garrisoned Kiska. When the 11th Air Force started bombing Kiska to soften it for the forthcoming landing, the PT boats organized an air-sea rescue service for downed airmen. Although only one rescue was made during the entire time, the presence of the boats boosted the morale of the bomber crews.

The PT boats also participated in the subsequent landings on Rat, Semisopochnoi Island, and finally the forbidding Kiska. During the assault on Kiska, it appeared that the PT boats would have some action at last after battling only the weather all these long months. Surprisingly, no enemy troops were found on Kiska. Later, they discovered that the entire Japanese garrison had evacuated quietly through the Navy's screen.

After the occupation of Kiska, both PT squadrons returned to Seattle for overhaul and were later sent to the Southwest Pacific. Despite the minor role played by the PT boats in the Aleutians, it did demonstrate the seaworthiness of these boats under adverse weather conditions.

At Massacre Bay, Attu in the Aleutian Islands, three Higgins PT boats and a PBY Catalina refuel from the USS *Gills* on June 21, 1943. *Photo courtesy of U. S. Navy*

PT boats at moorings inside new breakwater at Murder Point, Attu Island. *Photo courtesy of U. S. Navy*

2

Solomons

The Battle of the Solomon Islands

The first offensive action against Japan was the successful landing of United States Marines on Guadalcanal and Tulagi on August 7, 1942. Since the original PT Squadron 3 lost all its boats in the Philippines, a new Squadron 3 was formed which was again equipped with 77 foot Elco boats. It and Squadron 2 arrived at Tulagi towards the end of that year. During that time the Japanese cruisers and destroyers, known as the Tokyo Express, were making nightly runs down the Slot (the broad passage between New Georgia and Santa Isabel Island) to shell Henderson Field.

On the night of 14 October, several Japanese war ships were spotted by patrolling PT boats between Tulagi and Guadalcanal. Immediately, PT38 and the remaining two were at 200 yards as PT38 passed at full speed astern of the cruiser. The crew observed one torpedo hit. In the meantime PT60, attacking another ship, was caught in the searchlight of a Japanese destroyer and fired upon. Although slightly damaged, she ignored the destroyer and held her course until two torpedoes were fired. Not waiting to find out the result, PT60 retired at high speed and poured .50 caliber fire into the pursuing destroyer's bridge to knock out the searchlight. The chase was finally ended when two depth charges were dropped in the path of the destroyer. After this confused night action, the PT boats claimed one cruiser damaged and one probably sunk.

Thereafter, the presence of PT boats in the area so unnerved the Japanese Naval Forces that they temporarily stopped the bombardment of Henderson Field. In spite of the respite, the PT boats kept up the pressure in harassing any enemy shipping coming down the Slot. Due to the lack of radar at the time, the only indication that Japanese ships were nearby on a dark night was the roll and pitch of the PT boats caused by the wakes of the larger enemy ships.

It soon became apparent that the waters off Guadalcanal were too extensive to be patrolled adequately by the PT boats alone. Therefore, a group of Navy scout planes were assigned to assist PT boats in locating the Japanese shipping. One night a sea plane remained in the air too long and its gasoline ran out. It force landed in the water not far from several Japanese destroyers coming down the Slot. The pilot frantically radioed a PT boat nearby for a supply of gasoline. In a few moments, the PT boat glided smoothly alongside and the fuel was piped aboard the aircraft while both crews waited breathlessly, expecting a Japanese searchlight to flick on at any moment. After the transfer was completed, an argument ensued between the men on the PT boat and the pilot. The PT captain finally grew impatient and wanted to know what was going on. The boatswain yelled back, "This aviator guys want to pay us only 17 cents a gallon, but we're holding out for 20. "

Death in a PT boat could come swiftly. During the battle in the Savo-Esperance area that involved 15 Japanese destroyers and 11 PT boats, PT37 was hit right in the gasoline tanks. The tremendous explosion lighted the whole sky. There was only one survivor out of a crew of eleven.

On the early morning of July 20, 1943, three zebra striped PT boats of Squadron 10, returning from their night patrol, were strafed by four B-25 medium bombers. PT168 held her fire, but PT166 and 164 fired at the planes, thinking they were Japanese planes disguised with U. S. insignia. One B-25 was hit and crashed. All three boats were hit and PT166 caught fire and burned. Later investigation disclosed that the B-25 crews were mistakenly told that no friendly vessels were supposed to operate in that area. Another incident of mistaken identity illustrates how one vessel solved this problem. After a grueling patrol of Savo Island, one grim faced PT skipper reported that the previous night he had mistakenly fired all four of his torpedoes at a New Zealand vessel thinking it was a Japanese submarine. Fortunately all torpedoes passed safely under the shallow-draft craft. Several days later, the same New Zealand vessel came alongside a PT boat tender for fuel and fresh water. A huge sign was conspicuously placed on the side of her bridge reading "DON'T SHOOT – WE ARE ALLEGED ALLIES. "

With no more enemy destroyers coming down the Slot, the PT boats changed their mission to attacking enemy supply barges. Between July and August they engaged 105 enemy barges. During these attacks on the barges the PT boats were constantly harassed by Japanese floatplanes. Boat captains soon learned to slow their boats so the white wakes would not reveal their position. Even without the floatplanes, barge hunting could be very hazardous.

Barges usually hugged the shore to get protection from the shore batteries. With the dark background it was difficult to spot them. On the other hand, the PT boats themselves were visible against the horizon to the shore guns. Also, the PT boats carried only .50 caliber machine guns and 20 mm guns, which were no match with the shore batteries and ineffective against the heavily armored barges unless at point blank range. To increase fire power, torpedo tubes were replaced with automatic 37 mm guns for all boats. A few boats even had 40 mm cannons installed aft. Later squadrons had 40 mm cannons as standard equipment.

Teamwork between PT boats was important in attacking the barges, as demonstrated by the daring and almost disastrous daylight attack in Elliott Cove. With PT105 patrolling outside the cove as cover, PT104 and PT169 entered the cove. Spotting four barges behind a large camouflage net at the water's edge, they swung toward them and opened fire with their 37 mm guns. Immediately they discovered fire from enemy shore batteries on both sides of the entrance had them trapped in the cove. After completing their run against the barges the two boats, braving fire from both sides, raced for the entrance. As they emerged from the cove with shells landing all around them, PT105 charged forward, firing at the shore batteries to cover their tracks. Then she quickly reversed course and laid a smoke screen behind. All three boats headed for the open sea.

As the U. S. troops fought their way north up the Solomon Island chain, the PT boats also moved up. In November, while escorting a LCT to Treasury Island, PT167 came under attack from several Japanese torpedo bombers. In spite of the heavy fire put up by the PT boat, a plane came in at the boat straight and level with her propeller tips almost touching the water. When the plane passed over the boat after releasing her torpedo, her wing hit the boat's radio antenna and crashed into the sea. However, her torpedo hit home and a severe shock went through the entire boat but no explosion. Picking himself up from the deck, the 20 mm gunner of the PT boat fired at another torpedo plane, which was already on her torpedo run. The explosive shells registered along the cowling and fuselage and the plane crashed in the sea. She hit so close to the PT boat that the victorious gunner was drenched by the splash. After the attack, the crew discovered the torpedo had penetrated completely through the bow, leaving gaping holes on each side of the boat. Apparently the flimsy wooden construction of the PT boat hull did not offer enough impact to detonate the torpedo. Since the holes were above the water line and forward of the watertight bulkhead, the PT boat was able to continue her journey to her destination.

The Higgins boats, a different type of PT boat built by Higgins Industries, arrived in the Solomons for the first time in December. Their main duty was to strafe the Japanese shore installation in Choiseul Bay. The weather in January 1944 was bad, with heavy wind and rough seas. Despite the foul weather, the PT boats led the way for the successful landing at Green Island.

This was where Richard Nixon served as an Officer-In-Charge of William C. Specht, and led PT319 into the beautiful Rabaul Harbor for the purpose of reconnaissance. With poor visibility that day, nothing significant was found in the harbor. However, PT139 became the first allied vessel to enter Rabaul since its occupation by the Japanese. For the next few months the activities of the PT boats were confined to attacking any remaining barges that still tried to supply isolated Japanese troops on various islands. By May 1944, the battle of the South Pacific was over as far as the PT boats were concerned. All squadrons were either transferred to the Southwest Pacific under General MacArthur or joined the Seventh Fleet in the Philippines. Thus, the campaign in the Solomons ended.

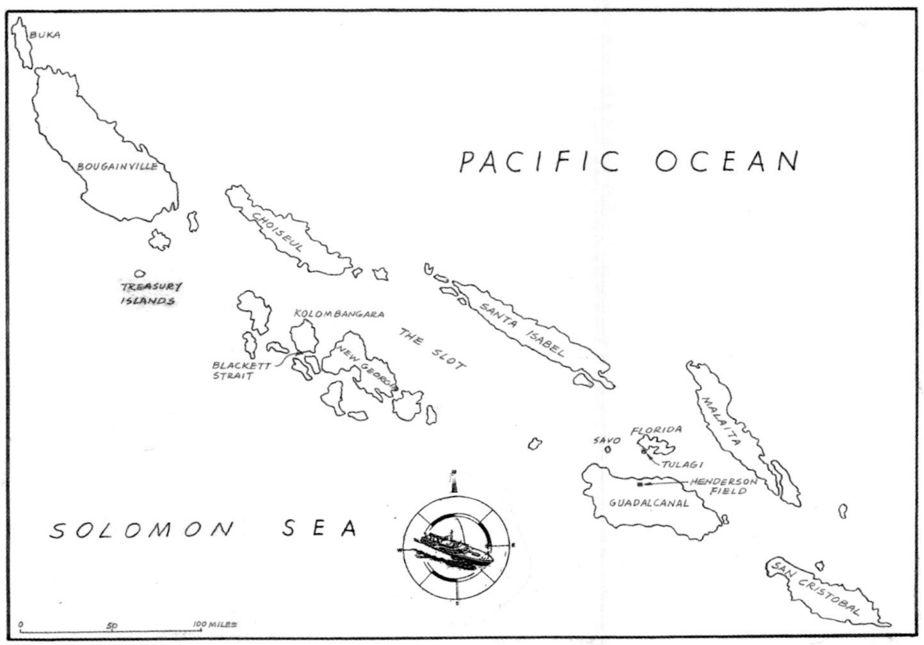

Map of the Solomon Islands

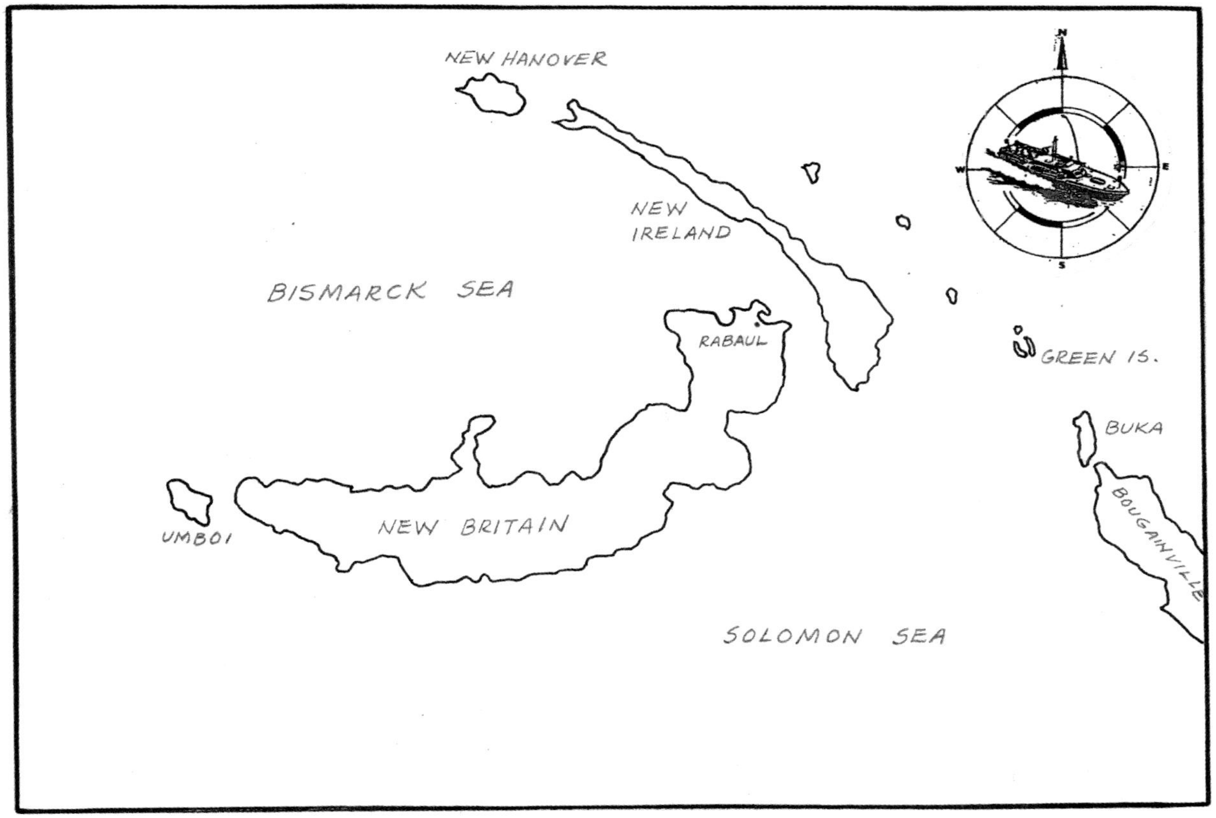

Map of New Britain

Tulagi PT bases 1, 2 and 8 on the Iron Bottom Sound near Guadalcanal. It was the headquarters for SoPac and opened October 12, 1942. This picture was taken in 1943. It shows both 77' and 80' Elco boats. *Courtesy of C. W. Faulkner*

PT47 being offloaded at Noumea, New Calendonia, November 1942. *Courtesy of the PT Boat Museum*

This photo is an Elco 77' that entered Tulagi Harbor July 1943. This photo was taken from USS *Nicholas* (DD-449). *National Archives*

Ron 2's PT47 being unloaded at Noumea, New Caledonia, November 1942. *Courtesy of PT Boat Museum*

With PT174 running alongside, this picture clearly shows the detail of the flag. *Photo courtesy of National Archives*

This is a photo of PT39 underway at East Coast on August 13, 1941. It was transferred to Ron 2, then on 27 July transferred to Ron 3. They were the first to arrive in the Solomons and engaged the Tokyo Express at Guadalcanal. *Photo courtesy of John C. Kennedy*

A picture of Ens. Bryant Larsen, skipper of PT109, with Squadron Commander Lt. Rollin Westholm on board as OTC (Officer in Tactical Command), who was at the wheel during the rescue operation of survivors of the *Northampton* sinking. *Courtesy of Jerry Gilmartin and Gene Kirkland*

Rare photograph of PT109 before Kennedy took command. On the night of 30 November 1 December, during the Battle of Espiritu Santo, Lt. Westholm's PT 109 rescued 94 men from heavy cruiser *Northampton*, sunk by the Japanese. *Courtesy of David Waples*

This is a photo of PT116 running at top speed out of Tulagi Harbour, July 1943. PT116 was commanded by Ens. Ralph Richards. It never saw combat with the Tokyo Express due to engine problems. *Photo courtesy of National Archives*

Ron 3 Officers: (L-r) Lt. Robert Searles, Lt. Bill Kreiner, Lt. Al Snowball, and Lt. John Searless, December 1942. *Photo courtesy of J. M. Searles*

Pictured are officers of Squadron 6 aboard PT124, May 1943. In the foreground are Ens. Alexander W. Wells and Lt. Clark Murray. In the background are (l-r) Ens. Richard North, Lt. Craig C. Smith, Lt. Clark W. Falkner, Ens. Bartholomew J. Connolly III, and Ens. B. P. Percy. *Courtesy of PT boats, Inc*

Robert Montgomery played the role of John D. Bulkeley in the movie "They Were Expendable. " In real life, he was in the Navy during WWII and saw action in the Solomons. He was XO of PT 107 and 114, Ron 5. *Courtesy of the PT Boat Museum*

PT 43, Guadalcanal, February 16, 1943. A PT boat beached behind the Japanese lines on Guadalcanal, following an engagement with Japanese destroyers off Savo Island. The boat was damaged the day following the beaching by U. S. Navy gunfire to prevent possible use by the Japanese. *Courtesy of Don S. Montgomery*

PT174 operating out of Rendova, Solomon Island, January 1944, shows the 40 mm gun on the foredeck. An officer named Whitney gave the 40 mm gun high marks against the enemy barge traffic. The caption is *Courtesy of Wayne Traxel Photo courtesy of David Waples*

Ron 10 PT boat at Viru Harbor, New Georgia, 1943. Note the rare zebra stripe used by Ron 10 (PT 163-174) in the Pacific. *Courtesy of Jim Mountcastle*

PT boats at Rendova PT Base floating dry dock. *Courtesy of G. G. Powell*

Lt. (jg) Sidney Dayton Hix. *Photo courtesy of Geary Sims*

On the morning of August 22, 1943, PT 108, skippered by Lt (jg) Sidney D. Hix, entered Webster Cove just west of the Japanese stronghold of Vila with PT125, carrying Army demolition crews for the destruction of the enemy installation. As soon as the boats were well inside, they were taken under heavy crossfire all around the cove. Lt. Hix, at the helm, was fatally wounded. He put the wheel hard over to withdraw before collapsing. Most of the crews were either wounded or killed. Somehow PT108 managed to clear the area of heavy fire. *Photo courtesy of National Archives*

"Lenny" Thom, executive officer on PT 109 under Jack Kennedy. He was played by Ty Hardin in the movie "PT 109." Thom was an All-American tackle at Indiana. Unfortunately, he was killed by a train shortly after the end of the war. *Courtesy of the PT Boat Museum*

On the night of October 6, 1943, the Japanese destroyer *Yugumo* was sunk by a US destroyer. On the morning of the 7th, PT108 searched the water to pick up Japanese survivors. On the extreme left is Eugene Foncannon, skipper, and crew after the rescue of the Japanese crew. *Photo courtesy of Tom Foncannon*

Note the uniform of the day. The skipper of PT157, Bud Liebenow, was wearing shorts and a white tee shirt that he wore for three months prior to this photo being taken, sixth from the right in front of the charthouse at Rendova, July 1943. To Liebenow's left is Commander Kelly, who led Ron 9, and earlier in the war was also Bulkeley's Number 2, who led a PT evacuation of MacArthur, his family, and his staff at Corregidor. *Photo courtesy of USMC*

This picture was taken from the stern of the Sea Plane Tender *Pocomo* in June 1942. The *Pocomo* picked up PT boats at Balboa and convoyed to the Galapagos Islands off the coast of Ecuador. *Courtesy of E. E. "Rich" Richardson*

On the night of May 5, 1944, PT245. Lt. (jg) C. A. Hastings with two other boats sighted three Japanese barges east of Rantan Island. Before an attack could be made more barges showed up on all sides, and a tremendous volume of fire was directed at them. Although one boat was hit, PT245 and the other boat made four attacks on the barges before retiring. *Photo courtesy of NAVSOURCE. org*

Unknown woman and Jerry Colona of the Bob Hope USO tour clown around on a PT boat that brought the troop to Green Island, Solomon. *Photo Courtesy of Frank Andruss*

This picture show the interior of a maintenance hut where guns were stored and repaired in order to get the PT boats ready for the mission. The maintenance men and the boat crews worked hard to accomplish this under very primitive living conditions and 100 degree temperatures. After a typical night mission, the PT boat would stop at the dock to drop off the skipper for the Intelligence meeting. The Exec. would take the boat to the fuel dock and get in line to be refueled. The gunner was to clean the twin .50 turret guns. Whether fired or not, they had to be stripped to remove the salt spray. If the gun had been fired, the gun barrel had to be replaced. The gunner also checked the .50 caliber ammo cans in the turrets to refill and checked for corroded ammo. Every couple of weeks the floor boards in the crew quarters and lazaretto were removed and the bilges were cleaned with lye. The Motormacs were always in the engine room with maintenance and repairs on the engines and the generator. Filling and checking fluids and gapping spark plugs were also part of this job. The Torpedo man was responsible for lowering the MK-13 onto the boat from a tender's crane, and the Quartermaster would check radar and radio units to make sure they were operational. Being a crew member on a PT boat was no easy task. *Photo Courtesy of Frank Andruss and CJ Willis*

PT157, commanded by Lt. Liebenow, is known for picking up Lt. Kennedy from a native canoe near Patparan, and also took part in the first action with Japanese surface ships at Rendova on July 3, 1943. It was under constant fire from enemy destroyers at close range. PT157 fired two torpedo salvos with no confirmation of a hit. *Courtesy of the PT Boat Museum*

The PT boats on Ron 5, during shake down and preparation for shipment overseas and doing formation maneuvers. Ron 5 saw action at Rendova, Vella Lavella, Treasury, Bougainville, Green and Emirau. *Photo courtesy of US Navy*

"Action in the Slot" by Tom W. Freeman, all rights reserved. PT 124, serving with Squadron six, runs for safety after firing three torpedoes at the Japanese Destroyer *Makigumo*. On the bridge of this little wooden PT boat was its skipper, Clark Faulkner, and his executive Officer, Leighton C. Wood. On this night, February 1, 1943, the Japanese were beginning a three day evacuation of Guadalcanal and had sent down a force of no less than sixteen Destroyers and three heavy Cruisers. They would be met by PT 124 and ten other PT boats. The Japanese Destroyer, having been hit by one torpedo, would later hit a mine and sink. Faulk was awarded the Navy Cross and Wood the Silver Star. *Copyright Tom W. Freeman, all rights reserved*

Leighton C. "Huck" Wood, seen here shortly after being called to active duty in January 1942. He was commissioned as an ensign in the US Naval Reserve and was ordered to the Motor Torpedo Boat Squadron Training Center at Melville, Rhode Island. After graduation Wood was assigned to Squadron Six, outfitted at the Brooklyn Naval Yard in 1942. He continued to serve with PT boats, fighting in the Solomon Island campaign, the Philippines, and Borneo. He earned five battle Stars and the Silver Star for his action. The savage battle of the Solomon campaign demonstrates the brutality of war. However, there is a human side of the story, as related by Huck Wood, Ron 6, 38, PT 124. He stated: "It was June 12, 1943, give or take a few days. I was the skipper of MTB 124 based at Tulagi, in the Solomon Islands. A day or so earlier Lt. Rollin Everton Westholm, class of 1934 (known to us as 'Westy'), had had the job of telling me that my Dad had been lost a few days before. At any rate, a second message came into our operations center at Tulagi instructing Lt. JG Leighton Wood to be standing by in the middle of Tulagi Harbor at, we'll say, 1100 hours, because COM DES Ron 23 wanted to speak with him. I was all of 22 years old, in the Navy for 18 months, had only seen duty in MTBs, and couldn't imagine what in the world this could be all about. About 1015 we were on station, lying to with our engines in idle, having spent a couple of hours cleaning up the boat and ourselves. Then, at about 1030 we saw four Fletcher Class destroyers standing in with a real bone in their teeth. They slowed somewhat upon entering the harbor. I came alongside the lead destroyer as it slowed further to about 5 kts. It never stopped! We tied up and I stepped aboard, saluting the quarterdeck. An officer, a commander, was there to greet me. He returned my salute as I asked permission to come aboard. The commander said 'Permission granted' and then asked, 'Is your name Leighton Wood, and was Captain Leighton Wood your father?' I answered 'Yes sir,' still standing essentially at attention. The commander held out his hand and said, 'My name is Arleigh Burke. I just wanted to tell you personally that your father was a good friend of mine and that his death was a real loss to the Navy. Now, son, I am sorry; but you must leave, as we are on a mission, and I calculated that there was just enough time, if we hurried, for me to speak to you of your dad and still make our rendezvous. Goodbye and good luck. '

"With that I stepped back aboard the MTB 124, said, 'Thank you, Sir,' and signaled my crew to cast off. We got clear as fast as possible.

"Minutes later, while my men were still asking me what had happened, DES Ron 23 and her commander were specks on the horizon. I had no deep thoughts at the time. We probably had to patrol that night, and the thought of trying to stop the Tokyo Express with 27 kt. torpedoes was most likely what I thought about that day. However, in retrospect, it was no surprise to me that COM DES Ron 23 later became the Chief of Naval Operations. He was capable of an extraordinary human act in the midst of combat war pressures. He figured out how to both get where he had to go to accomplish his mission and on the way console a young man whom he had never met, but who had lost a dad!" *Courtesy of Barbara Wood via Frank Andruss*

On the night of November 13/14, 1943, a full moon night, PT 154 and 155 were underway about 1. 5 miles from shore. The Japanese shore battery fired three shots in a bracket. The first went too far and splashed off the starboard bow. Thinking the splash was a bomb from a plane, Lt. Smith of PT 154 laid to, which was the procedure for night time bombing, as the wake of a speeding boat would light up the blue-green phosphorescence. PT 155 pushed full throttles and got out of harms way. One of the shots hit PT 154. The fact that the 3 inch shell hit the torpedo was fortunate. Otherwise, the shell would have penetrated the deck and down to the fuel tank and exploded. The boat made it back to base under its own power and it continued later on to Tulagi, where it was restored and returned to active duty. *Courtesy of Nathaniel Smith*

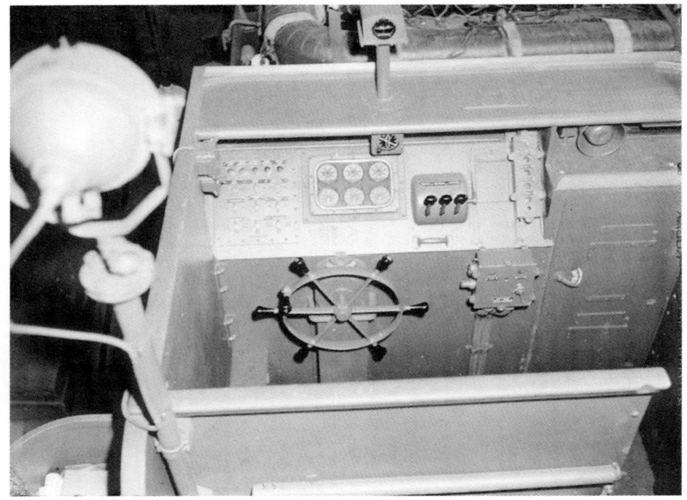

Shown is a picture taken in September 1943. It is PT 154 one month prior to being hit by a three inch shell. Note the shadow of the forward 20 mm gun and the 20 mm gun at the starboard turret. *Courtesy of Nathaniel Smith*

Pictured in a hat is Joe McLaughlin, who was killed instantly when the shell exploded. Shown at the helm is Hamlin D. Smith, who was unconscious for three days from the explosion but recovered. *Courtesy of Nathaniel Smith, Pat Rogers and Bill Nicholson*

On the night of November 13 and early morning of November 14, 1943, PT 154, with LT. (jg) Hamlin D. Smith as skipper, was lying off the south coast of Shortland Island. A 3 inch shell from a Japanese shore gun hit the after part of the port forward torpedo. The shrapnel killed one officer and two crewmen. The officer's name was Joe McLaughlin. Ex O. Lt. Smith (standing) and several men were wounded. The boat made it back to base on its own power and later to Tulagi, where it was repaired and returned to active duty. *Courtesy of Nathaniel Smith, Pat Rogers and Bill Nicholson*

Pictured is the damage from a 3 inch shell on PT 154. Pat Rogers, RMIc, is shown standing in the background. *Courtesy of Nathaniel Smith*

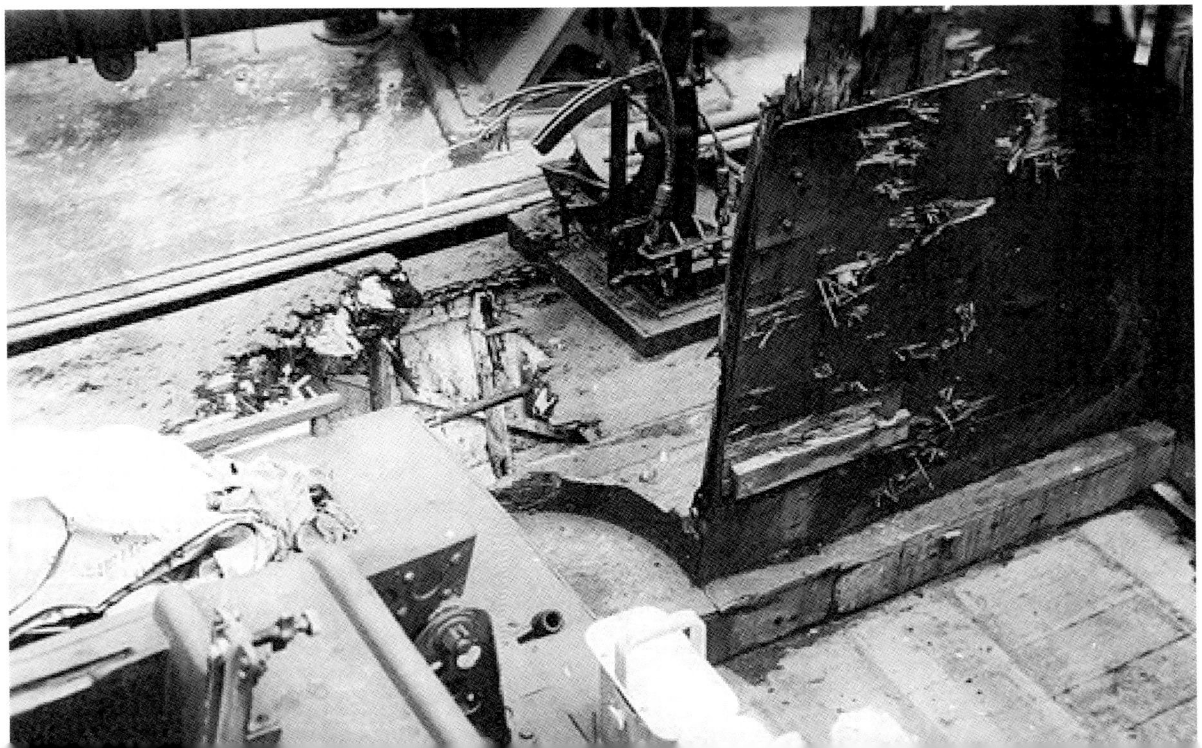

Note the damage of the wood partition by the shrapnel that killed Joe McLaughlin. To protect the crew on the bridge, Elco factory provided 1/4" armor plate around the cockpit. However, some boats had them removed to save weight and to allow easier access to the helm. *Courtesy of Nathaniel Smith*

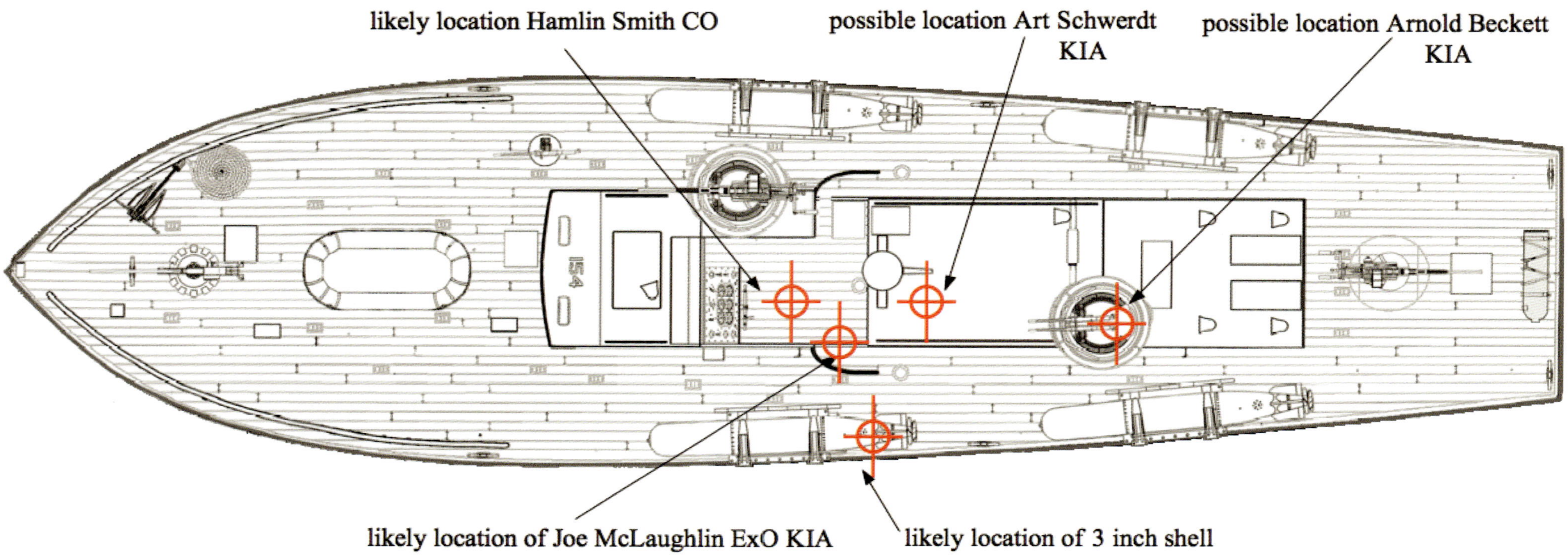

Shown is a drawing of PT 154's deck plan showing the location where the 3 inch shell hit. *Courtesy of Nathaniel Smith*

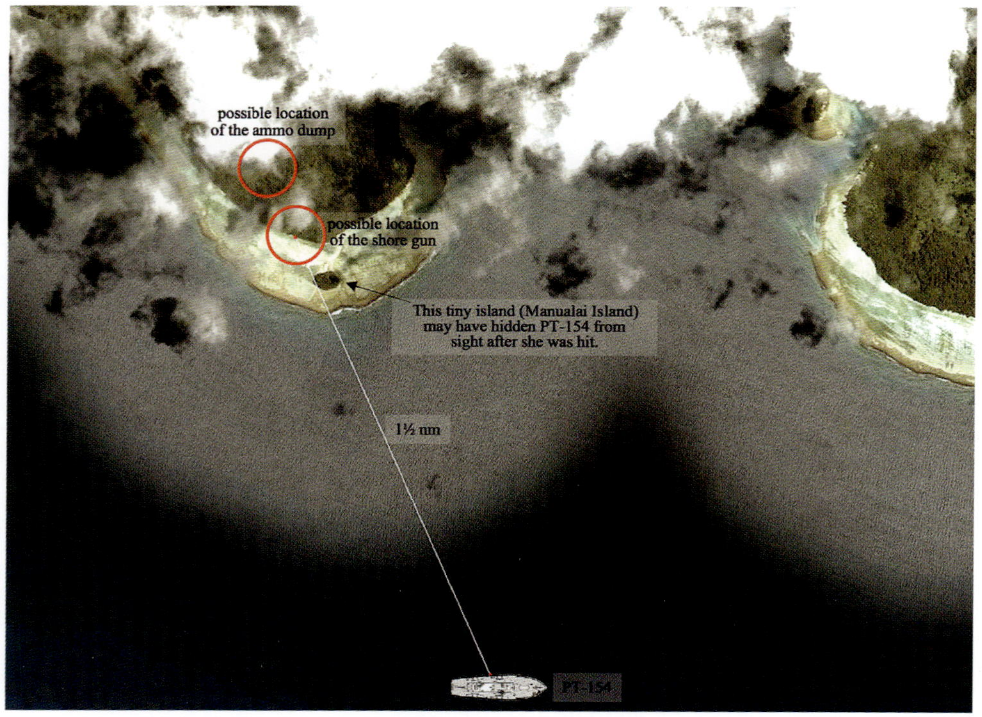

Shown is an aerial view of the Japanese shore guns and PT 154. Please note as the boat drifted forward, the line of sight from the shore guns would be blocked by Manualai Island, thus limiting the battery to firing only 3 shots before the boat was hidden behind the island. *Courtesy of Nathaniel Smith*

3

New Guinea

The Battle of New Guinea

New Guinea, shaped like a turkey and extending 1500 miles, is the world's most primitive and least-known island. The impassable jungle and rugged mountains limited all fighting to the northern coast. In order for the United States to liberate the Philippines, New Guinea must first be neutralized. With most of the Japanese forces committed to the Guadalcanal Campaign, General Macarthur's troops from Australia were able to clear the enemy from eastern New Guinea and made plans for the amphibious leaps east, along the north shore. To support these landings and to cut off the enemy supply barges, PT boats were much needed. To bring the PT boats to New Guinea, the tender *HILO* left Pearl Harbor in July 1942 with four PT boats on board. They arrived at their new base, Funafuti, in the Ellice Islands, in November. While there, the PT boats took part in a rescuing mission. A B-17, lost and running low on gas, was ditched in the ocean. 21 days later, a Kingfisher scouting plane on afternoon patrol reported sighting a yellow raft. PT21 immediately got underway and found the raft with one man in it. From him they learned of other survivors of the plane crash. Early the next morning, four PT boats were dispatched for a search mission. In late afternoon a Kingfisher located another raft. After it radioed in the position, the scout plane landed near the raft. With approaching darkness, all three men in the raft climbed aboard and the plane started a slow taxiing back to base 40 miles away. Within minutes, PT26 arrived at the scene and slipped smartly beside the plane. Two men, one of whom was Eddie Rickenbacker, the famous World War I ace on a special mission for the War Department, were quickly transferred on board and delivered safely to Gunafuti. The tender *HILO* and the four PT boats soon left for the southern tip of New Guinea. Together with PT121 and PT122 from Australia, they set up base at Tufi. On Christmas Eve, PT122 spotted a surfaced Japanese submarine, the I-22 type. Before the submarine could crash dive two torpedoes were fired at 1000 yards. One hit was registered, but the submarine remained afloat. Boring in closer, two more torpedoes were fired at 500 yards. The submarine was hit again, and this time she broke in half and sank silently out of sight.

Unlike warships, which fought the faceless enemy at long distance, the PT boats normally moved in close and sometimes came face to face with the adversary. On 1 March, an enemy convoy of 8 destroyers and transports carrying 70000 Japanese troops was sighted by reconnaissance planes. General Kenney's B-25s attacked the ships repeatedly, using the new skip-bombing method. By the third night, only 1 destroyer and 1 transport were still afloat. At that time, the PT boats moved in and sank the damaged transport. When the last destroyer was sunk by planes the following day, the Battle of the Bismarck Sea had ended. However, thousands of well armed Japanese troops from the sunken transports were still alive and adrift in life boats headed for shore. The PT boats moved in among all those bobbing heads and fired at them methodically. Individual swimmers were picked off with rifle fire, and rafts and lifeboats were blasted to bits by the powerful .50 caliber machine guns. Where swimmers were thick, depth charges were thrown at them. There seemed to be no end to this carnage. Attracted by the blood, great schools of sharks came from miles around to tear apart the dead and the dying. Finally the crews, worn out both physically and morally, got the job done and headed back to their base, leaving behind thousands of still bodies that stippled the glistening seas as far as the eye could see. This grim task caused some PT crews to vomit, but the large number of enemy soldiers had to be prevented from reaching shore to threaten the weak coastal defenses.

Several weeks after the Battle, two emaciated Japanese were found and brought to the PT boat base at Tufi. One was in fairly good shape, but the other one, identified as a medical officer from his paper, was seriously ill and died two days later. When PT142 was headed for Douglas Harbor, the body of the Japanese officer, sewed in a blanket and covered with a large

Japanese flag, was placed on the forecastle for sea burial. When deep water was reached, the funeral service was conducted by Commander Berry K. Atkins. During the service, a flight of Japanese planes was spotted heading for PT142. As the planes passed overhead no bombs were dropped and no guns were fired when the lone body slipped quietly into the calm waters.

The explanation of this strange act might be attributed to mistaken identity. With the Japanese flag clearly visible on the fore deck, the planes could have mistaken the boat as one of their own. A further twist of the story was the discovery that the supposed medical officer was but a simple soldier. When he was dying the real medical officer changed identity tags with him.

The closest fighting between a PT boat and Japanese barges took place on the rainy night of 15 March. PT114, with her engines idling, patiently laid in wait for the expected enemy supply barges. They could not see anything in the darkness until two barges bumped the side of the PT boat. Instinctively, the gunners swung their guns at the barges, but due to the closeness of the barges, they could not depress the guns enough to fire on them. Undauntedly, the PT boat pulled away while the aft machine guns were firing and sank one barge. The other barge somehow got caught under the bow of the PT boat and was pushed under by the weight of the 38 ton boat and sank out of sight. As the American ground troops moved east along the coast of New Guinea, the PT boats moved their base to Morobe. While there, the boats were mounted with 37 mm guns scavenged from obsolete P-39 fighters on their bow to provide armor piercing capability against some of the steel plated Japanese barges. Later, when Squadron 12 and 21 arrived, all their boats were equipped with 40 mm guns. Squadron 21 was not only the first squadron to have the 40 mm guns, but also the squadron with the most "muscle." Almost all their officers were either professional football players or other top athletes.

As experience was gained in attacking barges, new tactics formulated. The new doctrine called for PT boats to patrol closer to the shore, so that they had a better chance to detect the movement of the enemy barges and to catch any barges unloading on the beach. This, of course, also put the PT boats closer to the Japanese shore batteries. Another tactic was to have the boats in echelon formation while patrolling, with the boat farther offshore lagging behind the lead boat. So in case the lead boat should go aground, the other boat could tow her free of the reef.

With the troops pushing the enemy farther east, the PT boats continually advanced their base to Dreger Harbor in November, Saidor in March, Hollandia in May, Mics Woendi in June, and finally Amsterdam Island in July, in order to shorten the distance traveled in attacking Japanese barges. By November 1944, even before the Japanese had completely evacuated their forces from New Guinea, the PT boats were making ready for the final campaign of the Pacific, the liberation of the Philippines. Since the first arrival of PT boats in New Guinea, they expanded to 14 squadrons in 23 months. Along the north coast of New Guinea, hundreds of rusted wrecks of the Japanese barges could be seen as evidence of the bitter struggles to stop the Japanese inter-island traffic.

PT 156 underway at Finch Heaven, New Guinea, in July 1944. On the morning of August 17, 1944, PT155 and PT156 entered Dore Bay covered by one Beaufighter. They made 3 runs on 12 Japanese barges on the beaches of Mansinam Island. Six barges were destroyed. *Photo courtesy of US Navy*

This is a picture of Lt. Commander Barry Atkins, CO of MTB Squadron Eight. *Photo Courtesy of the National Archives*

PT boats in column formation in Hansa Bay, New Guinea, on March 7, 1944. *Courtesy of the US Navy*

This is a photo of PT66 heading out for a patrol off the New Guinea coast, July 1943. At this time the boat was a unit of Squadron Eight. *Photo Courtesy of the National Archives*

One of Ron 6 PT boats anchored at Kona Kope, next to the Asheville class patrol gunboat USS *Tulsa*, at their PT base. The PT boat has just returned from rescuing four crew members of A16, a Squadron 6 Lockheed Hudson piloted by Flight Lieutenant Ray Kelly. He was forced to ditch the plane in the bay when poor weather delayed them long enough for their fuel to run out. *Photo courtesy of Michael*

PTs 330 and 160 tied up at the FEMU YOG 23 for refueling near Mios Woendi, New Guinea, 1943.

Shown is an advance base located in Morobe, New Guinea. A crew member works on the aft gun turret spray shield, while a boom has been brought over to replace one of the boat's engines. Notice the recognition star that has been painted on the day room cabin roof. The star was placed there so it was easily seen by American pilots from the air. *Courtesy of Frank Andruss*

Pictured is Lt. (jg) Robert Lee Lanning, a PT 329 boat skipper. His squadron was commended by Vice-Admiral Thomas C. Kinkaid, Commander Allied Naval Forces, Southwest Pacific, for sinking nine Japanese barges during one night's action in the Southwest Pacific.

This picture shows the maintenance of a PT boat at Morabe, New Guinea.
Photo Courtesy of the National Archives

This photo was taken at Morabe, New Guinea. *Courtesy of the National Archives*

PT 185 in dry dock somewhere in the Pacific. *Courtesy of the National Archives*

PT331, nickname "The Wolf," with black crewman George Washington, CK-3 (Officers Cook 3rd Class), on board. Due to the condition at that time, very few African Americans served on board PT boats. His general quarters position was loader for the stern 40 mm gun. *Photo courtesy of Wayne Traxel*

Navy mud poured by Oneal J. Joshua. T. J. Lovvorn on left.

O'Neal J. Joshua was one of the few African Americans that served on board a PT boat. His name appears on Ron 12 roster. *Courtesy of the PT Boat Museum*

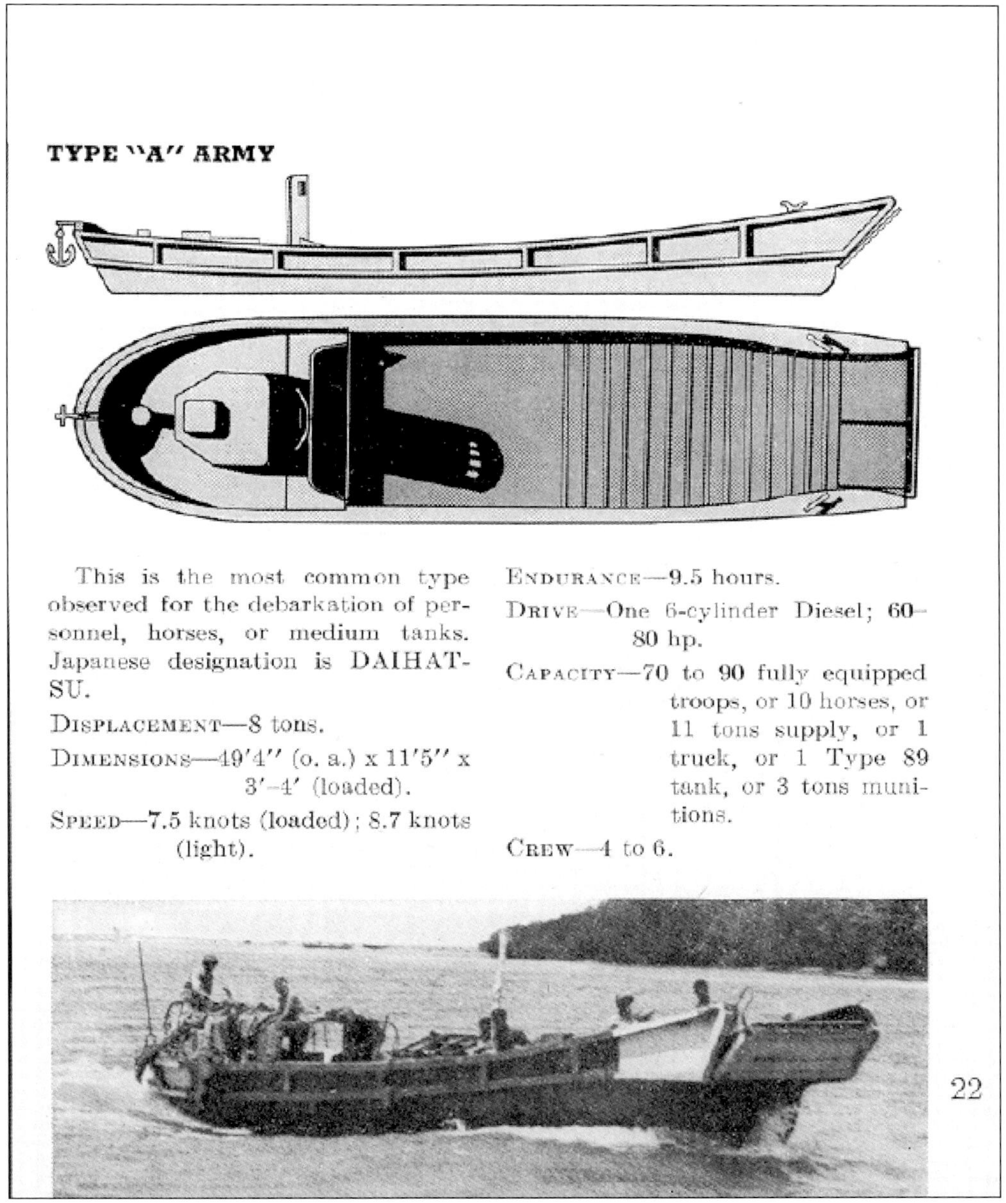

TYPE "A" ARMY

This is the most common type observed for the debarkation of personnel, horses, or medium tanks. Japanese designation is DAIHATSU.

DISPLACEMENT—8 tons.

DIMENSIONS—49′4″ (o. a.) x 11′5″ x 3′-4′ (loaded).

SPEED—7.5 knots (loaded); 8.7 knots (light).

ENDURANCE—9.5 hours.

DRIVE—One 6-cylinder Diesel; 60–80 hp.

CAPACITY—70 to 90 fully equipped troops, or 10 horses, or 11 tons supply, or 1 truck, or 1 Type 89 tank, or 3 tons munitions.

CREW—4 to 6.

22

Courtesy of the United States War Department via Jeff Davidson

This is an image of a PT boat prior to going on patrol at Morobe. Note the early 77 footer in the background. *Courtesy of the National Archives*

This is a photo of a typical PT boat base in the South Pacific. Note the radar dome on top of the mast for each boat; this indicates these are later boats. *Courtesy of the US Navy*

Ron 29, PT556 – 559, were equipped with the Elco Thunderbolt, a power-driven mount holding four 20 mm cannons. It was not effective against German F-lighters, but was successful against smaller targets. *Courtesy of Bill Maloney*

Four abreast, the PT boats ride in the oily water of the New Guinea anchorage, awaiting the night's call to action.

This photo displays the water front at Camp Taylor in Mios Woendiwas. This was the largest PT base in New Guinea. *Courtesy of the National Archives*

Ron 15 boats at Palermo. *Courtesy of Frank Andruss*

PT 307, 306 and 304 were on patrol when they were attacked by a German destroyer and a Corvette. PT 304 fired two torpedoes that brought the destroyer and Corvette within range of PT 306 and PT 307. PT 307 was hit with 20mm and 40mm rounds, but escaped when PT 306 blew smoke for cover. PT 307 lost 3 crew members and five were wounded, including Captain Paul F. Fidler. Captain Fidler brought his boat back to Bastia, 90 miles away, and refused to seek any aid until all of his crew were taken care of. *Courtesy of Gary Szot*

Ron 15 boats at Sardinia. *Courtesy of Frank Andruss*

USS *Savannah* was hit by a German radio-controlled bomb off Salemo, September 11, 1943. *Courtesy of the US Navy*

This is a photo of the crew on PT323, Ron 21, on board their boat. Lt. Emery N. Newton, skipper of the boat, is in the front row center leaning forward. *Courtesy of Kat Newton*

Lt. Emery M. Newton, skipper of PT323, at the cockpit of his boat off Biak. Note the captured Japanese prisoner huddled in blankets on the foredeck. He was captured with others in a native canoe south of Pak Island. PT323, under a different skipper, was destroyed by a Japanese plane in a suicide dive on December 10, 1944, with heavy loss of lives at Leyte Gulf. *Courtesy of Kat Newton*

THE SECRETARY OF THE NAVY
WASHINGTON

The President of the United States takes pleasure in presenting the PRESIDENTIAL UNIT CITATION to

MOTOR TORPEDO BOAT SQUADRON TWENTY-ONE

for service as set forth in the following

CITATION:

"For outstanding performance during the Huon Peninsula Campaign against enemy Japanese forces from October 1943, to March 1944 Highly vulnerable to damage from treacherous reefs and grounding during close inshore patrols, Motor Torpedo Boat Squadron TWENTY-ONE spearheaded a determined water-borne attack on the enemy, boldly penetrating hostile waters and disrupting barge traffic vital to the maintenance of Japanese strongholds in the New Guinea area. Dauntlessly exchanging gunfire with heavily armored gunboats and barges, airplanes and shore emplacements, the boats of Squadron TWENTY-ONE have successfully diverted hostile artillery fire to themselves in protection of Allied Land Forces; they have steadily destroyed the enemy's ships carrying troops, food and combat supplies; they have captured Japanese personnel and secret documents, landed scouting parties in hostile territory and effected air and sea rescue missions. Tenacious and indomitable in the face of superior fire-power and despite frequent damage to boats and casualties among personnel, the officers and men of Squadron TWENTY-ONE have fought gallantly and served with distinction in crushing enemy resistance in this strategically important area."

For the President,

James Forrestal
Secretary of the Navy

Courtesy of Kat Newton

A close up view of a shiny Mk XIII torpedo on board PT323 showing details of the exterior torpedo for serious modelers. *Courtesy of Kat Newton*

PT boats arriving at the advance base, Amsterdam Island.

Pictured is Camp Taylor on Mios Woendi. This was the largest PT base in New Guinea. *Courtesy of the National Archives*

Lt. Alfred G. Vanderbilt (left), of the famous Vanderbilt family, with Jim Costigan (center) and Kester Denman, Jr. (right), on board PT106, Ron 12, at New Guinea, 1944. On the night of 12/13 March, together with Lt (jg) Cyrus R. Taylor on PT193, they shot down a Japanese floatplane after it dropped a bomb astern of PT193. From the location of the searchlight, it is obvious that the picture was mistakenly printed in reverse. *Courtesy of the PT Boat Museum*

Lt. Alfred Gwynne Vanderbilt II was a member of the prominent Vanderbilt family. His great-grandfather, William Henry Vanderbilt, had been the richest man in the world. In World War II Alfred captained PT196, Ron 12, in the south Pacific, earning the Silver Star for bravery. *Courtesy of the PT Boat Museum*

4

Mediterranean

The Battle of the Mediterranean

In early 1943, the combined American and British army was pushing Rommel's Afrika Korps toward the coast of Tunisia. PT boats were needed to stop the German evacuation by sea. The forthcoming invasion of Sicily, a stepping stone for attacking the Axis in Italy and Southern France, provided an opportunity for PT boats to run against the German shipping.

The 13 Higgins boats of Squadron 15 arrived at Gibraltar in April 1943 from New York aboard two oilers. They established their first base at Bone, the most advanced port in Allies' hands in North Africa, under the command of the British Coastal Forces. The duty of the PT boats was to patrol the sea with the British MTBs within five miles of the coast. Their first action was in the Cape Bon area, where a PT boat and a MTB were making a sweep up the coast in the dark of night on 8 May. They spotted an enemy tanker against the dark background of land, but were too close to her to fire their torpedoes. Quietly they went around to the other side of the ship to line up for a beam shot. The PT boat fired one torpedo which headed straight for the tanker, leaving behind a white trail of bubbles. As the torpedo hit, the whole ship exploded violently, scattering debris all over the two boats. Upon retiring, they ran unexpectedly into two other British MTBs who hastily discharged tow torpedoes at them, thinking they were the enemy. Fortunately, both torpedoes passed under the boats. Within a month, the PT base was moved east to Bizerte, and patrols were made nightly to the west coast of Sicily getting ready for the landing.

During the dawn amphibious invasion of Sicily on 10 July, the PT boats patrolled the west flank of the task force against possible attack by the German E-boats. However, no enemy ship was encountered because the landing took the enemy completely by surprise. It was not unusual for people, other than the crew, to want to experience the thrill of riding in a fast moving PT boat. One Roman Catholic chaplain in particular is remembered fondly by the men of Squadron 15. He was on board one of the boats during a running gun battle with the German E-boats. When the confusion was at its height, with tracer bullets coming from all sides, the boat captain suddenly tripped over the padre, who was on his knees in the middle of the bridge praying for the safety of all aboard. Picking himself up, the captain exploded, "Father, we appreciate your prayer, but don't interfere with the action. If you want to pray, go below!"

In July Palermo, in northwestern Sicily, became the PT boats' new operation base. Their mission was to block enemy supply to Sicily and to prevent the enemy's evacuation from Sicily. The PT boats were best suited for this job, for they could skim through the enemy mine field with impunity due to their wooden hulls and shallow draft. The German F-lighters, 170 feet long and heavily armed, began to appear around the north shore of Sicily in increasing numbers. After several encounters with them, the PT boats learned not to fight them with guns but with torpedoes. On the night of 29 July, two PT boats engaged two F-lighters escorted by four Italian MAS 2 boats. The 2 Memento Auders Sempre, (MAS, meaning Remember Always to Dare) were speedy Italian boats that could easily outrun the heavily loaded PT boats; however, during this particular encounter, the two PT boats skillfully maneuvered within gun range of the MAS boats and strafed them with accurate machine gun fire. Before the F-lighters could operate their guns, six deadly torpedoes were streaming their way. The result was one F-lighter sunk and one MAS boat badly damaged and abandoned.

The German high command, realizing that further resistance on Sicily could cut off their entire army, began withdrawing their troops across the narrow strait of Messina to Italy. The Allies decided on an immediate invasion of Italy to keep up the pressure on the Axis. In September, the PT boats took part in the amphibious invasion of Salerno, Italy. They patrolled the Bay of Naples to screen the landing, and joined the Division Group in the capture of the Ventotene, an island west of Naples. LT. Douglas Fairbanks, Jr., who helped plan the various ways, such as setting off rockets and smoke pots at different beachheads to confuse the enemy as to the actual landing spot, was on board a PT boat at the landing at Ventotene. John Steinbeck, the famous novelist, who landed with Fairbanks, said later, "They told us that there were not Germans on the island, so we landed with flashlights lit and yelling to one another and the Germans thought we had an army with us. The captain and Douglas Fairbanks had nothing but Tommy guns and, so help me, they took the whole island." Later, Fairbanks continuously used PT boats for his many special missions.

As the American and British Armies moved north up the Italian peninsula, the PT boats also moved north to Capri, then Magdalena, and finally set up base at Bastia, north of Corsica. From there the PT boats patrolled the entire Gulf of Genoa.

One night in November, PT211 and another PT boat attacked an enemy ship escorted by three E-boats off the north shore of Giglio Island. PT211 fired four torpedoes within 450 yards. The night action report read, "As the first torpedo was fired, the tanker opened fire with one major caliber gun and several machine guns. Shortly after, the escort opened fire with 40 mm and 20 mm and the division increased speed to maximum and laid smoke. As speed was increased, one torpedo hit was observed at the tanker's bow. A few seconds later another hit amidships which caused an explosion. This was quickly followed by another which precipitated a violent explosion sending flames 150 feet into the air. The entire super structure of the tanker was thrown bodily into the air and it sank within a few seconds. The explosion was of such force that the PT boats were severely shaken at 800 yards. The escort ceased firing at this time. " Captured German records revealed that the tanker was actually a submarine chaser.

As more German F-lighters and E-boats moved down the coast of Italy to reinforce their troops fighting the advancing Allied Armies, the American PT boats and British MTBs worked as a team in attacking them. The PT boats, equipped with radar, were used as scouts and trackers in locating the enemy vessels. The MTBs, armed with better torpedoes and powerful 6-pounder guns, would go in for the kill. For the next 5 months these joint patrols claimed 15 F-lighters and 2 E-Boats sunk, and 3 F-lighter, 1 destroyer, and 1 E-boat damaged.

The PT boats often engaged the enemy at close quarters. On the night of 29 November, PT204 and another PT boat were patrolling near Genoa with heavy winds and less than 100 yards visibility. Suddenly, a German minesweeper loomed out of the darkness head on. PT204 turned hard left, but still hit the enemy vessel on the bow. The glancing blow pushed the PT boat away from the minesweeper, and intense gun fire was exchanged at point blank range. Although PT204 was riddled with bullets from stem to stern, not a man was hit.

Along with patrol duty, the PT boats also worked with the OSS in landing agents behind enemy lines. Late one afternoon a PT crew was startled to see boarding their boat a rather raffish group of young ladies escorted by a French female major with the build of a Notre Dame tackle. The only weapon she had were a pair of razor sharp knives strapped to the inside of her thighs. These "ladies," "all trained prostitutes," were Allied agents. This merry band was landed by rubber boats at the designated spot on the Italian coast and proceeded inland, presumably to carry out their dangerous mission in the perfumed bowers of the brothels.

In May 1944, Squadron 22 joined Squadron 15 at Bastia and Calvi. The boats of the new squadron were all equipped with torpedo racks and Mark XIII torpedoes, which were more reliable and faster than the old Mark VIII. All of Squadron 15's boats were also fitted with new racks, and a 40 mm gun was installed on the stern of each boat. In addition, their 1350 HP engines were converted to 1500 HP, thus increasing their top speed by 5 knots.

During the landing at Elba, a PT boat was assigned to escort a group of British LCGs (Landing Craft Gun) to attack and bombard the coastal batteries on the Pts. Dei Riparti, the southeastern extremity of Elba. The silencing of these guns was imperative, because they commanded the entire landing area, and hence could threaten the success of the invasion. By night, the PT boat led the LCGs to a position off the point and started the bombardment. The whole area was lit up by star shell illumination and heavy caliber fire was returned from the shore guns. Smoke laid down by the PT boat succeeded in diverting much of the enemy fire from the attacking LCGs. At dawn, the PT boat was sent close to shore to estimate the damage inflicted on the shore batteries by the LCGs' bombardment. When the PT boat came within half a mile of the point the shore batteries opened fire. She wasted no time in making her way seaward, and the LCGs managed to lay down another barrage on the shore batteries. After that the PT boat was sent in again to reconnoiter, and again the coastal guns opened up. This time they were firing in the direction of the invasion landing craft, for the landing had started. In order to divert the enemy's attention from the landing beaches, the PT boat opened fire with all guns into the mouths of camouflaged emplacements on shore. A David and Goliath duel ensued, and the PT boat, being outgunned, was forced to withdraw to avoid the concentrated enemy fire. This was repeated five times in broad daylight, until finally the German guns were silenced and the invasion could proceed.

During the invasion of Elba, the parts played by other PT boats were described in the war diary of radioman Bill Gallshand, who served on board PT562:

"We left our base in Galvi on June 14, 1944 and went to the other side of the island in a town called Bastia. We arrived the same day and started to put our boats into condition for the attack on the Isle of Elba, which is 27 miles from Bastia. Our Squadron 29 gathered alongside of Squadron 15 and 22. All in all there were 38 PT boats. On the night of June 16, we departed from Bastia and headed toward Elba. We ran patrol duty until the LCI's, LST's, LVEP's, etc. arrived at 0300. Then PT553, PT558 and PT559 headed for the isle to drop off the French commandoes they carried. No sooner had them headed away from the beach, hell broke loose, shrapnel, star shells lighting up the water for miles around. We could see the beach plainly and if we would have had newspaper along, we could have read them while sitting on the bow of our boat. Our officer remarked we are like riding down Broadway.

"At 0310, the PT's 554, 555 and 563 headed toward the beach and dropped their smoke pots. We saw it and at 0320, our zero hour, we headed in. When within half a mile from the beach, we fired our first salvo of rockets. The PT boat came to a halt when the rockets fired. Like a skyrocket on the Fourth of July, they sailed high into the dark sky, and after 30 seconds, which seemed like hours to us, the blazing trails died away. Then a pause of fifteen seconds more and our first salvo hit. Our target the radar station was blown to hell by subsequent salvoes and we had completed our assignment. We then started running a patrol between Elba, Genoa, Spezia and back. This was done to keep the Germans from landing reinforcements. At 0400, the main body of men headed for the northern shore of Elba. The next day, the French, English and Italian flags were flying on the island."

Two other PT boats found two MAS boats near Elba and opened fire at them at 800 yards. The enemy retreated at high speed and returned fire with their 20 mm guns. At full throttle, the PT boats gave chase for 10 miles in a running gun battle. Just as the MAS boats started to pull away from the pursuing PT boats, hits finally registered on one of the MAS boats. Both PT boats bored in and concentrated on pouring fire into the disabled craft. The entire crew of the Italian boat abandoned ship and was taken prisoner.

As an experiment, four boats (PTs 556 to 559) of Squadron 29 were equipped with the new Elco Thunderbolt gun mount, a power-driven mount holding four 20 mm cannons. The effectiveness of the new guns against the well compartmented F-lighters was doubtful; however, their withering fire against smaller ships was more than adequate.

On the night of 15 July, PT558 and two other boats left their base at Corsica to patrol the Liaurian Sea. They spotted a German patrol craft near Nice and made a firing run at 500 yards. The continuous tracers streaming from PT558's Thunderbolt, like the beam of a searchlight, hurled destructive projectors at 1800 rounds per minute at the patrol craft. As the PT boats pulled away, the perforated patrol craft was out of control. PT558 turned around and pulled alongside the disabled vessel for boarding. They found two men dead and one badly wounded out of a crew of seven, and counted about seventy 20 mm hits. After the wounded man and all documents were taken aboard PT558, the badly listed and punctured craft was sunk by 40 mm fire from the other two PT boats. Erratic torpedoes, particularly the old Mark VIIIs and occasionally the new Mark XIIIs, were a constant source of worry and frustration.

Patrolling off the coast of Italy, PT204, -213, and -304 sighted two German F-lighters, and deployed into echelon formation for torpedo attack. Before they could fire any torpedoes the enemy opened with heavy and accurate fire. The two lead boats, PT204 and PT213, fired torpedoes at a range of about 1500 yards and turned away. Suddenly, a torpedo from PT304 was seen to run under PT213 and slammed into the stern of PT204. Miraculously there was no explosion. On board PT204, the boat captain at first thought they had hit a rock, but on sending a man aft to investigate found to his horror a torpedo with its warhead firmly imbedded in the lazarette, the rear compartment. The torpedo man quickly jammed a rag into the vanes of the torpedo impeller to prevent it from arming itself. They retired under a smokescreen and limped back to base with the punctured PT204, whose personnel were a shade greyer the next morning, for they never knew during the entire 80 mile trip back when that warhead might go off.

It was later discovered that the exploder was better than three-quarters armed, and that with only 25 more turns of the impeller it would have blown up the boat. Six hours before the invasion of Southern France, which took place on August 15, 1944, 16 PT boats were used to put commandos ashore. The main assault landings once more found the PT boats screening the assault forces against enemy ships, while also maintaining a blood bank shuttle between Calvi and the beachhead. PT boats of Squadrons 15 and 29 were ordered to station themselves near the coast so that the planes towing American troop gliders for the invasion could use them as navigation markers. As the planes came over one of the gliders was accidentally released. With not enough altitude to make it to land, the fully loaded glider started her descent down into the sea. Realizing her predicament, the PT boats got underway to get in position for a rescue operation. As the glider hit the water with a splash she floated with her wing above water. The troops managed to get out and climbed on top of the wing. By that time PT209 was alongside with boarding nets over the side. On board PT562, which was standing by during the rescue operation, Seaman 1st Class Michael Kalausky took the pictures. When Southern France was in the hands of the Allies, the boats of Squadron 15 were transferred to the British Coastal Forces under land-lease in October. Squadron 29 was withdrawn from operation, and part of the boats were given to Russia, while the rest were shipped back to the United States. In the summer of 1945 Squadron 22, assembled at Oran, was then also shipped back to the United States.

During the PT squadrons' two year operation in the Mediterranean, their losses were 4 boats destroyed by mines and 5 officers and 19 men killed in action. They had fired 354 torpedoes, sunk 38 enemy vessels, and damaged 49. While in joint operations with the British MTBs they had sunk 15 vessels and damaged 17. This was quite a record for such small boats.

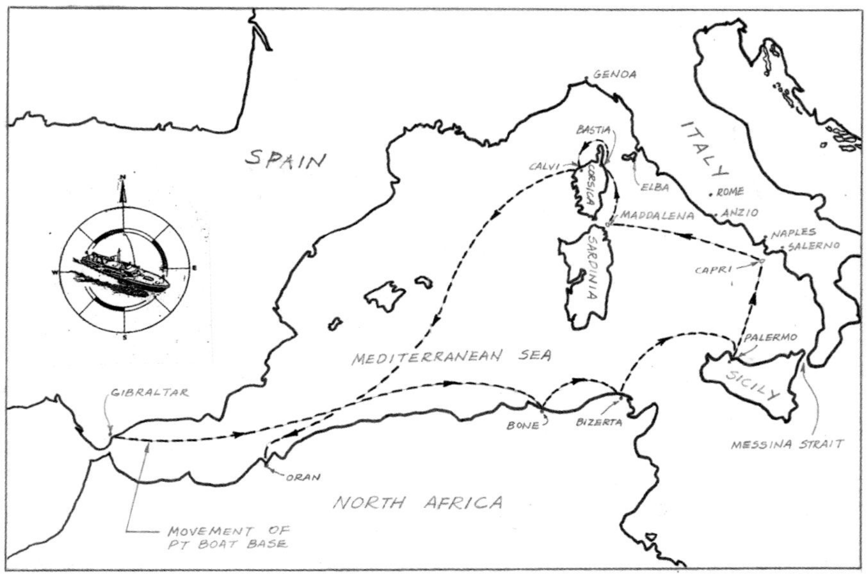

A map of the Mediterranean Sea. *Photo courtesy of the author*

A photo of an unkempt and dirty Ron 15, PT201. On January 28, 1943, PT201 transported General Mark Clark from Naples to Anzio. When the PT boat was 25 miles below the Anzio it was hit by friendly fire from the minesweeper SWAY. LT (jg) George E. Peterson, the skipper, was wounded. Ens. Paul R. Benson maneuvered away at full speed until out of range and arrived at Anzio without further mishap. *Courtesy of the PT Boat Museum Message Board*

During the invasion of Southern France, PT 209 rescued soldiers from a crashed glider accidentally released from the tow plane. Seaman 1st Class Michael Kalavsky took this picture from PT 52 during this rescue operation. *Courtesy of Michael Kalavsky*

Italian MAS Boat. *Courtesy of the Italian Navy*

Pictured is PT 303, Ron 22, south of France, heavily damaged high above the waterline. It was in no danger of sinking. *Courtesy of the PT Boat Museum*

PT 559 with its Elco Thunderbolt under cover, leaving the seawall at Corsica. *Courtesy of Michael Kalavsky*

Mike Kalavsky is shown on board PT559. He was the official photographer of Ron 29. Note the six kill marks on the bridge. *Courtesy of Mike Kalavsky*

Pictured is Ron 29, 554 boat in the Mediterranean. This photo was taken by Seaman 1st Class M. Kalavsky, a noted photographer. *Courtesy of the PT Boat Museum*

Two Elco boats docked at a port in North Africa. These boats were stripped of torpedoes and depth charges in order to improve performance. *Courtesy of the PT Boat Museum*

Ron 15's PT214 plowing the water somewhere in the Mediterranean Theater. PT214 engaged German F-lighters and destroyers many times. *Courtesy of Frank Andruss*

Lt. Commander Stanley M. Barnes was awarded the Navy Cross for extraordinary heroism as Commander Motor Torpedo Boat Squadron 15 during the Tunisian and Sicilian Campaigns. *Courtesy of the PT Boat Museum*

This picture shows Ron 29 at Bastia, Corsica. *Courtesy of Mike Kalavsky*

On the night of June 4, 1944, the mission of PT210 (Higgins), with LT. (jg) Harold J. Nugent on board, was to land six commandos on the southern coast of Elba. After completing the mission, PT210 patrolled the area for German E boats. Suddenly PT210 was under heavy fire from 88 mm and 20 mm guns. The first blast tore off the right side of Nugent's binoculars that he was wearing around his neck. It also tore through the bridge and scored a direct hit on the engines. PT210 returned fire immediately. By then an E boat and two F-lighters could be seen moving rapidly toward the stern. The engines were quickly repaired and they got under way. Surprisingly no one was hit. They joined up with PT209 to resume patrol. *Courtesy of Will Day*

Here is LT. Nugent grinning next to the boat damaged during the Elba shootout. Note the splintered wood from the cannon hits. *Courtesy of Steve Nugent*

This photo depicts PT210 underway before she was damaged by heavy fire from a German E boat and F-lighters. *Courtesy of Will Day*

This PT210 name plate was brought by Larry Smith in an antique mall at Minnesota. Recently it was given to Lt. Nugent's son Steve. *Courtesy of Larry Smith*

A photo of PT210 after it received extensive repair in June/July 1944. Note the paint color difference on the side of the boat. *Courtesy of Jim Stanton*

Bill Donovan (head of OSS) standing on a PT boat next to Lt. William F. Toohey and the crew of Ron 15. They operated with the British Coastal Forces. *Courtesy of Gary Szot*

Lt. Commander Douglas Fairbanks, Jr., member of the Beach Jumpers, aboard PT 309 en route to the Island of Vis to set off rockets and smoke pots at the beachhead to confuse the enemy. *Courtesy of Bill Pleasants*

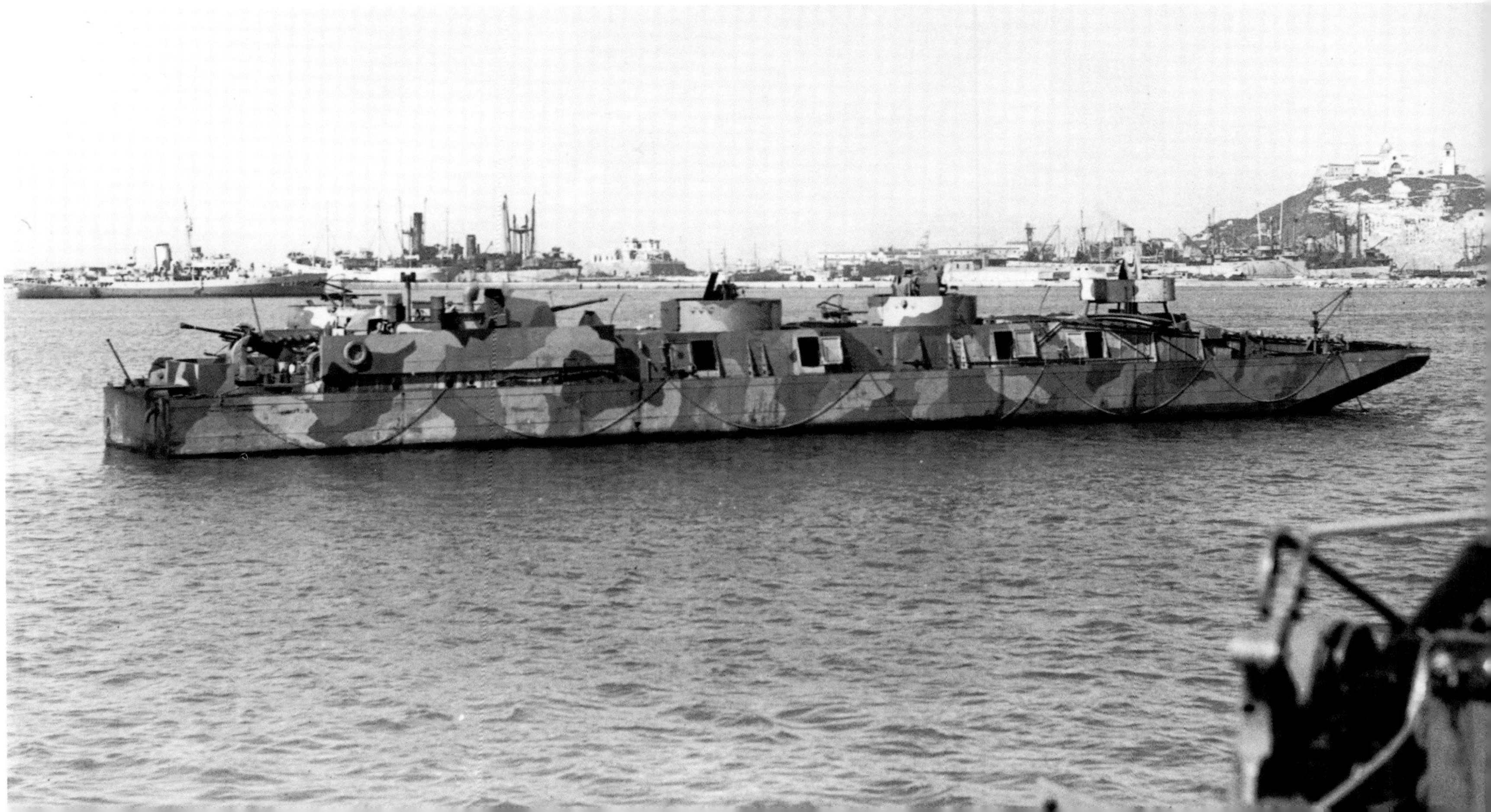

German F-lighter, or Flak ship, at Ancona. *Courtesy of the Imperial War Museum*

On the night of June 20, 1944, PT308 and PT309 captured by the two Italian MAS boats after a running gun battle. 14 crew members were made prisoners, including the commander of the Italian MAS flotilla. *Courtesy of the PT Boat Museum*

British MTP-385 headed out to sea. This type of boat worked closely with PT boats in attacking German F-lighters. *Courtesy of Vosper*

"When the beach jumpers landed on the Pontine island of Ventotene in September 1943, Fairbanks chased a German up the beach and then witnessed the surrender of the Faschisti as other Allied forces were landing. After a day's standoff, the remaining Germans surrendered. Fairbanks (standing, right) and company captured a Nazi flag from a German gunboat, (Douglas Fairbanks, Jr., collection)"

5

English Channel

American PT boats were used in the English Channel in the spring of 1944, when the Office of Strategic Service (OSS) requested these boats to pick up their agents on the French coast. The newly formed Squadron 2, commanded by Lt. Comdr. John D. Bulkeley of Philippines fame, reached Dartmouth, England, in April 1944. All boats were installed with special navigation equipment to help them in finding their objectives on the French coast. During May and November of that year, Squadron 2 completed 19 missions for the OSS, picking up and taking out agents and equipment right under the German guns. So well executed were these clandestine undertakings that not once did the enemy spot the PT boats.

On D-Day, June 6, 1944, the newly arrived Squadron 34 took part as screen forces in the invasion of Normandy. The PT boats escorted minesweepers to clear a sea-lane to the beaches. Under the cover of naval bombardment, they approached within half a mile of the French coast. However, except for some rescue operations and carrying high ranking officers to the beachhead, D-Day turned out to be a milk run for the PT boats. However, according to Bud Liebenow of PT199, who had rescued 65 sailors (using resuscitation to recover 5 of 6 sailors who had stopped breathing) from certain death in the Channel's waters after their ship, the USS *Cory*, was sunk. Liebenow also said they were up (awake) for nearly four straight days.

The comment of Quartermaster First Class Robert G. Center–who was on board PT499 "Miss Kate" (named after Kate Smith)–about D-Day illustrates the typical missions carried out by the PT boats on that fateful day. He says:

"As the great fleet began the crossing, we raced out ahead and around both sides of the spearhead like border collies herding sheep, constantly on the lookout for enemy ships which we never saw. Our draft was so slight that we could roar right across mine field. However, a couple of minesweepers did hit the mines and blew up during the crossing.

"Once the ships were safely escorted across the channel, we were ordered to anchor in a particular area, approximately one mile off Omaha Beach, and furnish supplementary anti-aircraft cover. The sky was absolutely covered from horizon to horizon with C-47 transport planes towing gliders in high and the planes alone returning low.

"Later, we were ordered to pick up airmen shot down, which we did. We also picked up a German pilot, who appeared to have a badly damaged back. We had a little Pomeranian dog for a mascot name Salty. We had always assumed that if we ever picked up an enemy soldier. Salty would guard him. However, when we gently placed the wounded German flier on a bunk, he had no more than settled back before Salty had snuggled up beside him. Some watch dog!

"After the beach was secured, our squadron was assigned patrol duty off the channel islands to keep munitions and supplies from reaching the German troops stationed there. It was during one of the duty trips to the islands that PT499 was almost shelled out of the water. We had accidently gotten within range of the shore batteries on one of the islands when they opened up. Since we were half way through the opening between the islands we couldn't turn back. So we zigzagged and varied our speed until we were out of range.

"We never encountered any German E Boats. It was easy enough to identify them at night though. Their tracers would be streaking parallel to the water, while out's would be alternately parallel then about up 45 degrees. This is due to the difference in hull design between PT boats and E boats. The PT boat, with planning hull, would skip from wave to wave. This made it hard for the gunners to hold the guns down on target. The E boat, with displacement type hull, could cut through the waves of the rough channel water and made it a more stable gun platform but a slower boat. "

The second morning of the landing, the USS *Tide* was sweeping for mines suspected to have been planted by German E boats during the night near St. Marcouf. Suddenly, a magnetic mine exploded under her, lifting the entire ship several feet out of the water. With the dead and wounded all around the sinking ship, PT509 was there immediately to assist the rescue. The PT boats, with their wooden hulls and shallow draft, were the only vessels that could more safely navigate through the minefield.

Throughout the month of June, with more PT boat squadrons arriving, they patrolled to the northwest of the invasion beaches toward Cherbourg, which was still occupied by the Germans, hoping to catch them evacuating by sea. However, no contact was made.

In August, the PT boats were transferred to Portsmouth to work with the British destroyers. They learned the technique of using a destroyer to coordinate the attack. The destroyer, with a superior radar, could vector the PT boats in the attack by radio.

On the foggy night of 8 August, five PT boats were patrolling with a British destroyer west of the Island of Jersey. Just before dawn, the destroyer radioed PT509 the range and bearing of a German R boat, or minesweeper. After maneuvering into position, PT509 fired one torpedo at 700 yards but missed the target. To ensure a hit, she charged in at a good clip to within 200 yards and opened fire with her machine guns. The murderous return fire from the heavily armed minesweeper was intense and accurate. One shell hit the cockpit of the PT boat, killing the helmsman and put the boat out of control. A second shell exploded in the chart house, setting it on fire. Still moving at high speed, she rammed the minesweeper broadside and wedged firmly into her.

From the deck, the Germans blazed away with small arms and tossed hand grenades down on the helpless PT boat. Radioman John L. Page, severely wounded from the fire and collision, managed to crawl out of the burning chart house during the skirmish. He staggered painfully past the bullet riddled body of the bow gunner toward the slippery blood soaked fore deck. The German tossed him a line and hauled him aboard their ship. Page was half conscious when he felt the heat of the blast as the PT boat exploded, killing the remaining crew still on board. The German sailors frantically pried loose the flaming hulk by using crowbars and boat hooks. After first aid treatment Page was taken to St Helier, where he was questioned by the Gestapo agents concerning radar on board the PT boat. He was too badly shot up to answer and was then taken to a hospital, where a German surgeon performed many operations on him for the next 5 months. Released to the prison camp, Page was finally liberated, 4 months later, upon the surrender of Germany.

As Allied troops occupied much of the French coast, Squadron 2 was shipped back to the States and Squadrons 34 and 35 were transferred to the Russians. The boats of Squadron 30 triumphantly escorted the first Allied ships into St. Peter Port, on the Island of Guernsey. Then they too were shipped back to the States.

Ron 35, PT513, in the English Channel contacted 6 enemy R-Boats and one E-Boat on August 1944. With visibility of 150 yards, the action lasted for only 2 minutes. PT513 suffered hits during this brief encounter. *Courtesy of the US Navy*

PT 510 and two boats led by Lt. James C. Mountcastle attacking three E-boats coming out of LeHavre. The boats scored several 40mm hits and the E-boats retired back to the harbor. *Courtesy of Frank Andruss*

PT505, Ron 34, England. On June 7, 1944, Lt. William C. Godfrey's PT505 ran over a mine while chasing a submarine. This caused heavy damage to the entire boat. After jettisoning all guns and torpedoes, PT507 towed the PT505 to anchorage in the lee of St. Marcouf Island. *Courtesy of Frank Andruss*

Secretary of the Navy James V. Forrestal and Major General Alexander M. Patch, commanding general of the 7th Army, on a Higgins class PT boat approaching the newly won beaches in Southern France on D-Day, plus one. On the right is Rear Admiral A. Lemmonier, who commanded the elements of the French Navy that participated in the assault. *Courtesy of the PT Boat Museum*

This photo shows one of Ron 34's boats at the dock at Portland Bill. Ron 34 was in time to take part in the operation on D-day. The PT boats of Ron 34 were to escort minesweepers to clear a broad sea lane to the beaches. *Courtesy of the US Navy*

PT502 of Ron 34 docked at Portland Bill, England, with measure 13 overall Haze Gray with dark blue decks. *Courtesy of David Waples*

Pictured is a head on view of a heavily armed PT boat of Ron 34 ready to dock at Portland Bill, England. *Courtesy of David Waples*

Ron 35 boat returning to base in England with a German prisoner. *Courtesy of the PT Boat Museum*

Pictured are Ron 30 boats, Cherbourg, France. The 6 boat squadron operated out of Cherbourg after its capture. Boats in the European Theater normally were painted grey with a white star on deck for aerial identification.

On the night of August 10/11, 1944, PT 515 was hit by enemy fire while attacking a trawler, R-Boat, and E boats. *Courtesy of the US Navy*

Pictured is a late war S-1000 type German E boat with the armored bridge. They engaged US and British PT boats occasionally; however, their targets were Allied shipping. *Courtesy of the Imperial War Museum*

PT 461 underway en route to an assault area in the English Channel. *Courtesy of S. E. Garner*

A pair of PT boats of Ron 30 in close formation in the English Channel from June 1944 to June 1945. *Courtesy of the PT Boat Museum*

6

Philippines

The Return to the Philippines

The return to the Philippines began first with the occupation of the weakly-garrisoned Morotai Island, which lies roughly halfway between New Guinea and Mindanao, on September 15, 1944. The PT boats of Squadron 33 were patrolling the landing area when one U.S. carrier plane was shot down by enemy ground fire. The heroic rescue of the pilot in Wasile Bay, less than 200 yards from the Japanese occupied beach, by PT489 and PT363 awarded them the Lt. A. Murray Preston the Congressional Medal of Honor. The citation reads, "For conspicuous gallantry and intrepidity at the risk of his life above and beyond the call of duty as Commander Motor Torpedo Boat Squadron 33 while effecting the rescue of a Navy pilot shot down in Wasile Bay, Halmahera Island, less than 200 yards from a strongly defended Japanese dock and supply area, September 16, 1944. Volunteering for a perilous mission unsuccessfully attempted by the pilot's squadron mates and a PBY plane, Lt. Commander (then Lt.) Preston led PT489 and PT363 through 60 miles of restricted, heavily mined waters. Twice turned back while running the gauntlet of fire from powerful coastal defense guns guarding the 11 mile strait at the entrance to the bay, he was again turned back by furious fire in the immediate area of the downed airman. Aided by an aircraft smoke screen, he finally succeeded in reaching his objective and, under vicious fire delivered at 150 yard range, took the pilot aboard and cleared the area, sinking a small hostile cargo vessel with 40 mm fire during retirement. Increasingly vulnerable when covering aircraft were forced to leave because of insufficient fuel, Lt . Commander Preston raced PT boats 489 and 363 at high speed for 20 minutes through shell splashed water and across minefields to safety. Under continuous fire for 2 1/2 hours, Lt. Commander Preston successfully achieved a mission considered suicidal in its tremendous hazards and brought his boats through without personnel causalities and with but superficial damage from shrapnel. His exceptional daring and great personal valor enhance the finest traditions of the United States Naval Service. "

During their stay at Morotai the PT boats made nearly 13,000 patrols, destroying over 200 barges and, most important, isolated 37,000 well armed Japanese troops on neighboring Halmahera by blockade throughout the Philippines campaign. In October, 45 additional PT boats arrived from New Guinea. Before their arrival, they were refueled at sea from the tenders in order to have enough gasoline to take part immediately in the Battle of Surigao Strait. The objective of the Japanese Task Forces involved in the Battle of Surigao Strait was to destroy the American supply shipping in Leyte Gulf. Task Force I was under the command of Vice Admiral Mishimura, and steamed north in column toward the Strait on the night of 24 October. It was comprised of 2 battleships, 1 heavy cruiser, and 4 destroyers. As they approached the strait, they were attacked by PT boats hidden in darkness. With only tracers and gun flashes visible, the damage to the Task Force was not certain. As the enemy ships entered the Strait and sailed north, they were incessantly attacked from both sides by PT boats stationed all along the strait. When the column almost reached the northern entrance, the PT boats received radio messages from US destroyers to break contact and clear the area. Quickly retiring to the sides, the PT crews watched the destroyers coming down the Strait to take over the attack. At the same time, the enemy column was met by the American cruisers and battleships of Rear Admiral Oldendorf using the classic naval tactics of "crossing the T." This maneuver was executed so that the guns of every American ship crossing the T could effectively shell the enemy ships leading the column. By means of this deployment, Task Force I was almost completely destroyed before they could turn around. During the shelling, PT323 moved in and made three torpedo runs against the destroyer ASAGUUMO and one torpedo hit her in the stern. Damaged and dead in the water, she was later sunk by American cruisers and destroyers.

Task Force II, with 3 cruisers and 4 destroyers, under the command of Vice Admiral Shima, was 30 miles behind Task Force I. Not knowing the defeat of Task Force I, the column steamed toward the southern entrance of the Strait. Suddenly the cruiser ABUKUMA was hit by a torpedo from PT137, killing all the crew in the radio room. The damage reduced her speed to only 19 knots, which forced her to drop out of formation. For the remainder of the passage through the strait, the Japanese ships' positions were accurately reported to the heavy American forces by PT boats still stationed along the Strait. Time and again, the enemy ships revealed their position by firing at the attacking PT boats. As the column reached the head of the Strait, Admiral Shima's flagship collided with a retreating cruiser of Task Force I. With his flagship damaged and Task Force I routed, Admiral Shima commenced full retreat. After the battle, only one Japanese destroyer of Task Force I escaped. The harassing action of the PT boats contributed substantially to the defeat of the Japanese Task Forces. In this engagement, 30 of the 39 PT boats participating were under enemy fire and 10 were hit. A 4.7 shell tore away the 37 mm gun from the bow of PT152 and fatally wounded the gunner. PT493 was lost after receiving three direct hits.

The day after the Battle, General Douglas MacArthur returned to the Philippines at Tacloban, Leyte, aboard PT525. The following day, the Japanese launched their air attacks of unprecedented fury against the PT boats in Leyte Gulf. Suicide dives were employed against the PT boats for the first time. On the afternoon of 10 December, four enemy planes attacked four PT boats underway for their patrol station. PT327 and PT323, leading the formation, went immediately into evasive action. The standard procedure was for the boats to turn hard and peel off in opposite directions. However, as PT327 turned one way for some unknown reason, PT323 also turned the same way. One plane came in low, just missing PT327, and cut PT323 almost in half with her wing, killing the captain and the second officer. The two P-61 pilots on board PT323 decided to never ride on a PT boat again. A second plane, following every turn of PT532, started to make a determined suicide dive. As the plane closed to 500 yards, PT532 quickly turned hard left and the plane hit the wake and exploded only 25 yards behind the boat.

As the US ground troops pushed inland on Leyte, the Japanese brought in supplies and reinforcements from Cebu by barges and destroyers. The PT boats, based at Leyte Gulf, had frequent encounters with them. On the night of 11 December, radar revealed a destroyer in the vicinity of the west coast of Leyte. Two PT boats skillfully worked their way between the beach and the destroyer so as to make themselves less visible, and the destroyer was silhouetted against the light horizon. When they moved in to about 1000 yards from the enemy they launched their torpedoes. Two hits were scored, sending up a column of water followed by flash and flame. Later the destroyer sank.

On 15 December, during the troop landing at the southeast corner of Mindoro, PT boats and several escort vessels entered Mandarin Bay and came under attack by four Japanese planes. Three were shot down by the combined fire of all the vessels. The fourth was shot down in flames by PT221 as it swooped in for a suicidal stern attack. About that time the Japanese Shinyo boats made their appearance in the Mindoro area. It was simply a small motorboat piloted by one man, loaded with high explosives in the bow to detonate against any ship by contact. The PT boats made a series of successful strikes on their hideouts and destroyed a large number of them amongst the islands. As a result, few American ships were lost to the Shinyo boats. Due to the ferocious suicidal air attacks, the Mindoro campaign was most costly to the PT boats in the Southwest Pacific, both in lives and boats. However, the PT boats did stop the Japanese inter-islands. As a result, few American ships were lost to the Shinyo boats.

On January 9, 1945, the US Sixth Army landed in Lingayen Gulf to begin their reoccupation of Luzon. The PT boats started their nightly patrol around that area immediately. They found little activity because the enemy made no more attempts to reinforce their troops at Luzon. During the subsequent months PT boats were used to blockade northern Luzon to prevent enemy evacuation.

In March, PT134 and PT248 entered the heavily defended harbor of Cebu City. When they got within half a mile of the wharf, several guns opened up on them from shore. The PT boats turned around and fired back. They destroyed several barges and set two freight cars on the wharf ablaze before clearing out of the harbor. While the battle for Manila was still raging, a coordinated airborne and amphibious attack, the most difficult of all military maneuvers, was put into motion. Remembering that the Japanese had lost almost half their initial amphibious assault force in attacking the heavily fortified Corregidor in 1942, paratroopers were dropped from C-47s to seize key positions and disrupt the enemy's defenses. Anticipating that some paratroopers would miss the small drop zone, which was surrounded by trees and steep cliffs, several PT boats were assigned for pick-up and rescue missions. After strafing the shore batteries, the PT boats circled the water close to shore with their crews intently watching the slow descent of the paratroopers. Because the leading planes had disgorged paratroopers from an altitude of 550 feet instead of the planned 400 feet, the descent drift became greater and sent some men onto the cliffs south of the drop zones, while others barely hit the narrow beaches below the bluffs. Under intense fire from enemy snipers, a score of paratroopers were picked up by rubber rafts as the PT boats waited only 50 yards from shore. The parachute drop diverted the enemy's attention from the landing craft moving on Corregidor and confused the defense forces. By the time they had recovered their wits sufficiently to take meaningful action, the US troops had secured their objectives with light losses. After Corregidor was taken, General MacArthur triumphantly returned to it on board PT373, a much improved version of the type he used leaving three years before; thus fulfilling his pledge of "I shall return."

The few remaining Japanese soldiers on Corregidor refused to surrender and tried in vain to escape by swimming to Bataan. PT327, under the command of Lt. Kenneth B. Sharpe, was patrolling the area and spotted two Japanese in the water. Pulling along side of them, the crew asked them to come aboard. One soldier committed hara-kiri in the water by stabbing himself with a short Samurai sword he was carrying. The other soldier, also eager to die for his Emperor, pulled the sword free from the lifeless body for use on himself. Due to the excitement and the slippery blood soaked handle of the sword he dropped it. Lt. Sharpe, who always wanted a Samurai sword for a souvenir, watched it sink slowly out of sight. If the water was not so deep, he probably would have dived overboard. The second Japanese finally drowned himself by diving under the boat.

One dark night, on the way to rendezvous with other PT boats north of Leyte, PT327 was caught suddenly in the search light beams of three Japanese destroyers. Instantly, the entire deck of the PT boat was lit up like daylight and was fired upon. It didn't take long for her skipper, Lt. Sharpe, to realize that they were outclassed and outgunned. Turning his boat around, he beat a hasty retreat. It seemed to take forever for the boat to pick up speed, and by then, still pinned by the search lights, a 5 inch shell landed 10 yards off the port side of the boat, sending up a white spout. By turning the boat toward the spout, the next shell landed where the boat would have been if going straight. Like a jack rabbit running away from a hunter, the PT boat zigzagged between spouts. Finally, the order to turn on the smoke screen was given from the bridge and dense smoke hid the PT boat from the view of the destroyers. Apparently thinking the PT boat was on fire, the destroyers poured all their fire into the smoke while the PT boat slipped away into the darkness. After his heart beat slowed down a little, Lt. Sharpe asked the two 18 year old gunners why they didn't open fire with their 40 mm gun while pinned by the search light. The white faced and frightened sailors replied, "Sir, we don't want to give our position away."

El Fraile, a small reef island south of Corregidor, had been turned into a formidable fortress before World War II by the US Army. Atop the reef, a concrete battleship-shaped citadel with 20 feet thick walls and top was constructed. After the recapture of Corregidor, the crew of a PT boat, thinking Fort Drum (as it was called) was abandoned, made an unscheduled reconnaissance. The Japanese garrison of 70 naval troops held their fire until seven US sailors made their way a third of the way through the corridors. Suddenly a Japanese machine gun opened up, killing one officer. The landing party made a hasty withdrawal to bring back reinforcements. Because the fort's four 14 inch guns and four 6 inch guns had never been repaired by the Japanese during their occupation, a US LSM was able to get near the fort and landed troops on top of it using a specially rigged drawbridge-like ramp. While the infantry covered all openings, engineers pumped 3000 gallons of oil into an open vent and lowered dynamite into another opening. After everyone got clear, a deafening roar shot great clouds of smoke and flame skyward. A series of secondary explosions threw steel plates and chunks of concrete a thousand yards out to sea. Thus was liberated the last of the islands of Manila Bay.

With the last battle after the capture of Corregidor, the Philippines Campaign was drawing to a close. The next step was the invasion of Borneo, southwest of the Philippines. The PT boats were moved to Tarakan Island, northeast of Bornea, in April 1945 to sink enemy luggers and to strafe the beaches to prevent the Japanese from repairing the obstacles that were destroyed by US Engineer Assault Teams in preparation for the invasion. The new 5 inch rockets carried by PT532 were used for the first time in the Pacific. The results were 1 lugger sunk and two others damaged. With the beaches cleared of obstacles, the landing on Tarakan Island met with little resistance. The next few minutes found PT boats sinking a dozen or more enemy small craft. When the Japanese resistance on Tarakan Island came to an end, the PT boats captured and killed many who were trying to escape in dugouts and canoes.

As the PT boats patrolled the northeast coast of Borneo, they strafed the enemy's beach defenses. Tracers ricocheted from wood and concrete, knocking off large chunks of obstacles and killing troops. This marked the final action for PT boats before the cessation of hostilities of WWII.

When the shooting war was finally over, PT boats were used in accepting the surrender of Japanese forces on the many islands in the Philippines. The most important of which was carrying Lieutenant General Ishii, Commanding General of Japanese Forces of Halmahera, to Morotai, where the 37,000 troops and vast amounts of equipment, including 900 cannons and 600 machine guns, were surrendered. Such was the force that the PT boats had blockaded for nearly a year.

Pictured is PT194 refueling from USS *Wachpreque* on October 20, 1944, en route from Borneo to Leyte Gulf. On July 22, 1945, PT174, with LT (jg) Robert L. Baker in command, made a daylight strike on Paloe Bay, Celebes. Four large fires could be seen 30 miles at sea. *Courtesy of the National Archives*

This is a photo of a Ron 12 at Leyte, in the Philippines. *Courtesy of Frank Andruss*

Pictured is Ron 12, PT146, at Samar Island Drydock. *Courtesy of Earl Richmond*

Pictured is Ron 12, PT195, underway at San Pedro Bay, Philippines. She was credited with shooting down one enemy plane. A quad machine gun was mounted on the port bow of this boat. *Courtesy of Ted Walther*

Ron 12 boats at Ormoc, Leyte, 1945. *Courtesy of Frank Andruss*

PT490 with General MacArthur and staff on board across from Negros Island to Iloilo, Panay Island, P.I., 1942. *Courtesy of Russ Blaise*

On November 19/20, 1944, PT495 made a successful sweep of Ormoc Bay and the Camotes Islands. Five barges and several luggers were sunk or damaged. An enemy plane dropped a bomb next to PT495, killing one man and wounding others. *Courtesy of National Archives*

PT 375 with rescued paratroopers that landed in the water off of Corregidor.
Courtesy of the PT Boat Museum

PT 579, Ron 39 – stern view – vessel in delivery condition, March 2, 1945.
Courtesy of Elco

PT 66 "Cheetah" Base 17, 77' Elco, Samar. Note the shark jaw on the bow.

Pictured are two PT boats idling in Leyte Gulf during a bombing attack. The liberty ship in the left background was subsequently hit by a Japanese plane that was shot down. *Courtesy of the US Navy*

PT 523, with PT 524 and 526, were guarding the eastern entrance to Surigao Strait. Lt. Commander Francis D. Tappaan, on board PT 523, picked up radar targets and closed in to fire two torpedoes before it took fire. Later Tappaan attacked two battleships and three destroyers. *Courtesy of the PT Boat Museum*

Pictured is PT131 preparing for the upcoming battle of Sarigo Strait. During the battle, its radar picked up the advancing Japanese task force. Note the additional weapons on board. *Courtesy of the National Archives*

PT321 picks up Japanese survivors after the battle of Surigao Strait. *Courtesy of the US. Navy*

A US concrete bunker built in the defense of the Philippines. The bunker had 2 16 inch guns and was protected by 10 inches of concrete. This photo was taken by PT373 as she was going by. *Courtesy of Frank Andruss*

On the morning of July 14, 1945, PT163, led by Lt. Roger V. Waugh, took part in destroying an enemy radar station on Balabalagan Island, in the Little Peternoster Group. *Courtesy of Henry Beazley*

Rear Admiral Selman Stewart "Biff" Bowling, USN, who commanded all the PT boats in the seventh fleet operating in the Admiralties and throughout the Philippines and parts of Borneo. He commanded 245 PT boats and some 10,000 men, and earned the Silver Star Medal as a squadron leader at Guadalcanal and the Legion of Merit and a Distinguished Service Medal. He graduated from the U. S. Naval Academy in 1927. *Courtesy of the PT Boat Museum*

Pictured is a PT190 in the Philippines, 1945.
Courtesy of the US Navy

PT492, Ron 33, was in the Leyte area on the night of 11/12 December, with Lt. Melvin W. Haines on board, and led PT490 to attack a Japanese destroyer. They worked the boats between the destroyer and the beach, making the PT boats hard to detect. They launched 6 torpedoes 1,000 yards from the target and got two hits. *Courtesy of the US Navy*

This is a photo of PT125 in dry dock along tender USS *Pontus*, AGP-20, off Samar, June 19, 1945. *Courtesy of Henry Beazely*

On board PT132, the Alamo Scouts performed a mission on Mindanao. Alamo Scouts were the 6th Army's top secret reconnaissance and raider unit operating behind Japanese lines. *Courtesy of the US Navy*

The crew of PT379 supported the Alamo Scout mission around Luzon. *Courtesy of the US Navy via Bill Rakin*

"Daytime Mission" – Taken by Erskine Van Houten on PT 523, Ron 36, July 1945, off the coast of Borneo, near Tarakan. PT 529 is off to port. *Courtesy of the PT Boat Museum*

Pictured is a damaged Japanese lugger on Leyte, a typical target for the PT boats. *Courtesy of Milt Dondt via Wfzimmerman*

Lt (jg) Brown, left, received the Bronze Star and Purple Heart for his action at the Battle of Surigao Strait on the night of October 25, 1944. During the Battle of the Surigao Strait PT493, nicknamed "Carole Baby" (Ron 33), with Lt. (jg) R. William Brown on board, was stationed in the middle of the strait with two other boats when they picked up four radar targets. PT493 tried to launch a torpedo, but it hung in the rack and was forced to retire. A 4.7 inch shell passed through the boat, then another shell tore through the engine room. A third shell hit the charthouse canopy, killing two men and wounding five, including the skipper. Ens. Robert E. Carter regained control of the boat and beached it. *Courtesy of Donald Brown*

THE SECRETARY OF THE NAVY
WASHINGTON

The President of the United States takes pleasure in presenting the BRONZE STAR MEDAL to

LIEUTENANT RICHARD WILLIAM BROWN
SUPPLY CORPS
UNITED STATES NAVY

for service as set forth in the following

CITATION:

"For heroic achievement as Commanding Officer of PT 493 in action against a superior force of enemy Japanese combat vessels during the Battle of Surigao Straits on the night of October 25, 1944. Although wounded by shrapnel and suffering flash burns when his boat was struck by 4.7-inch projectiles which killed two men and wounded several others, Lieutenant Brown directed the heavy machine-gun fire of his boat against the searchlights and bridges of the Japanese vessels. Under continuing close-range heavy fire when serious flooding started during the action, he ordered the executive officer of the boat to head for the shore and, disregarding his own wounded condition, went below to the engineroom to supervise damage control, keeping the craft afloat to reach shore on her own power. Successful in reaching shore as the last engine was put out of action by flooding, Lieutenant Brown was instrumental in getting all hands off before the boat sank and in keeping them together until picked up by another PT Boat. His heroic conduct throughout this action against tremendous odds was in keeping with the highest traditions of the United States Naval Service."

Lieutenant Brown is authorized to wear the Combat "V"

For the President,

Secretary of the Navy

Pictured is the commander of PT493, Lt. Richard W. Brown.
Courtesy of Donald Brown

Pictured is PT493 underway, heading for the Surigao Strait. *Courtesy of the US Navy*

Pictured are Ron 33 boats getting ready for a night mission. Note the covered 20 mm gun at each side of the chart house and at the bow. *Courtesy of the US Navy*

Of all the PT boat action reports in World War II, none is more dramatic than the rescue at Wasile Bay, South West Pacific filed by A.M. Preston, who received the Congression Medal of Honor. The following is the actual Action Report.

ORIGINAL

ACTION REPORT

USS PT 489

NO SERIAL 17 SEPTEMBER 1944

RESCUE MISSION OF A FIGHTER PLANE PILOT SHOT DOWN IN WASILE BAY, ON 16 SEPTEMBER 1944 - REPORT OF.

PT'S DEPARTED MOROTAI TO RESCUE AVIATOR DOWNED IN WASILE BAY, HALMAHERA, SOUTH WEST PACIFIC.

90686

OFFICE OF NAVAL RECORDS AND LIBRARY

102

MOTOR TORPEDO BOAT SQUADRON THIRTY-THREE
% Fleet Post Office, San Francisco, Calif.

FC8-33/A12/sq
CONFIDENTIAL

17 September 1944.

From: Ensign Herbert A. GREGG, D-V(G), USNR., Commanding Officer (Temporary) PT 489.
To: The Commander-in-Chief, U. S. FLEET.
Via: The Commander, Motor Torpedo Boat Squadron 33.
The Commander, Motor Torpedo Boat Squadrons, SEVENTH Fleet.
The Commander, SEVENTH Fleet.

Subject: Rescue mission of a fighter plane pilot shot down in Wasile Bay, on 16 September 1944 - report of.

1. This action was a rescue mission of a fighter plane pilot shot down in Wasile Bay, by Japanese anti-aircraft fire. The mission was completed.

2. At 1350 ITEM, on 16 September 1944, PT's 489 and 363 got underway for Wasile Bay on a rescue mission of the downed pilot, course 180 T, speed 1600 R.P.M., Lieutenant Arthur M. PRESTON, O.T.C. on board the PT 489. The boats continued on this course for 21 miles then changed to 220 T. This was done to avoid reported Japanese mine fields and enemy shore batteries on the eastern shore. At 1515, visual contact was made with a PBY. Radio communications could only be maintained through the command ship. The boats had no other air cover at this time. At a distance of four miles from the narrows, a large caliber gun on the western shore opened up. Course was changed to the eastward to avoid this fire. This took the boats across the reported enemy mine fields. In a few minutes three heavy caliber guns opened up on the eastern shore. The boats then turned to retire in a northerly direction, maneuvering to avoid enemy fire. Soon after the boats were out of range, the fighter plane cover appeared, but a second attempt was forced back by the shore guns.

3. At 1600, the boats came about to attempt to enter the bay again. The planes commenced strafing gun positions on either shore of the entrance. At 1605, guns on both banks opened up again, much more accurately than on the first attempt to enter. At 1620, both PT's were through the entrance and in Wasile Bay, still under fire however. At this time, another gun inside Lolobata Point commenced firing. The pilot was reported to be down near this point, but the boats were unable to contact him there so continued into the bay. A TBF laid smoke along the shore. At this time, heavy fire was being directed at the boats from both the northern and southern shore of Wasile Bay. The same TBF then vectored the boats toward the downed pilot at a point several miles back to near a second jetty. This was at 1720. As the boats approached the pilot, the TBF laid more smoke to cover the pilot's position.

90686 FILMED 12 0557

-1-

Of all the PT boat action reports in World War II, none is more dramatic than the rescue at Wasile Bay, South West Pacific, filed by A. M. Preston, who received the Congressional Medal of Honor. The following is the actual Action Report.

In April 1945, the PT service received an order from General MacArthur to rescue the Sultan of Ternate, Iskander Muhammad Jabir Syah, who before the war had governed the area under the influence of the Dutch. On 8/9 April, PTs 364 and 178 with Z force, consisting of Australian, Dutch, and native scouts on board, headed for the Island of Hiri, Ternate. The Z force rescued the Sultan, his two wives, his eight children, and a retinue of courtiers and relatives. On 11 April the same two boats picked up all of them and returned them safely to base. This is the first and only time that PTs were used to transport a harem. *Courtesy of Mike Hillis and the PT Boat Museum*

Shown is PT 178 on a mission to rescue the Sultan of Ternate from the Island of Hiri.

The "Peacock Lounge" (PT 84) patrolled the western coast of Borneo near the end of WWII. *Courtesy of Scott Cunningham*

PT 84 Skipper James K. Cunningham at the cockpit of "Peacock Lounge" on the way to Kuching, Borneo, to accept the Japanese surrender. *Courtesy of Scott Cunningham*

On board "Peacock Lounge" (PT 84) are Australian and American officers waiting for the surrender of the Japanese prison camp at Kuching, Borneo, in September 1945. *Courtesy of Scott Cunningham*

Jim Cunningham, commander of PT 84 "Peacock Lounge" in the Pacific, where he participated in seven battle campaigns, including the invasion of Borneo. *Courtesy of his son, Scott Cunningham*

Crewman of PT 344 touching up a Ron 25 logo at Morotai. The equipment mounted near number 344 is a Navy Pelous used for navigation. *Courtesy of Robert Hostetter, who was the XO on PT 344*

Ens. Robert Hostetter, XO of PT 344 in Isabella. PT 344 did not see action before the end of WWII. *Courtesy of Bob Hostetter*

7

Early PT Boats

The Navy's first PT boat, the Scott-Paine PT 9. *Courtesy of the PT Boat Museum*

Part of an early squadron of 70 Elco PTs on a formation run in the Atlantic. The succeeding group of ELCOs were 77' in length, followed by 80 footers, which continued to be built by the Electric Boat Company, Elco Naval Division, at Bayonne, N.J.

Pictured is PT7, an Elco 77 footer, underway at speed. *Courtesy of Elco*

This is a photo of several Elco 77' running in formation off the East Coast. *Courtesy of Elco*

Pictured is PT8 underway with the Statue of Liberty in the background during a training operation. Note the covered torpedo tubes and .50 caliber machine guns for protection against the spray of sea water. *Courtesy of the US Navy*

Ron 2 PT boats in column formation.

Builder's trial of PT 621 on the Long Island Sound.

This is a photo of Ron 2 at Biscayne Bay, Miami, Florida, 1941. *Courtesy of Ted Walther*

On December 31, 1940, the Elco 70 foot boats of Ron 2 made the trip to Miami to join the first PT boat tender USS *Niagara*. Then they headed for Cuba for shakedown cruises. In March, Ron 2 returned to New York and transferred most of the boats to the British under lend-lease. PT18 helps tow the stricken PT11 back to the USS *Niagara*. *Courtesy of Frank J. Andruss*

PT11 tied up to the USS *Niagara* after being towed in.
Courtesy of Frank J. Andruss

PT10, replicas of the Scott-Paine model, making a trial run on the East Coast.
Courtesy of Gene Kirkland

Ron 2, PT19, placed in service December 31, 1940, placed out of service July 2, 1941, and transferred via lend-lease to Britain. *Courtesy of the National Archives*

Pictured is PT18 alongside the stricken PT11 along the Cuban Coast. *Courtesy of Frank Andruss*

This is a photo of 70 foot Elco PT15, 10, and 19 resting in Miami, Florida. *Courtesy of Frank Andruss*

Pictured are 21" torpedo tubes aboard Elco boats of Ron 2 at Washington Navy Yard in December 1940. Note the un-muffled exhausts. They also lack smoke generator. Dewandres. *Courtesy of National Archives*

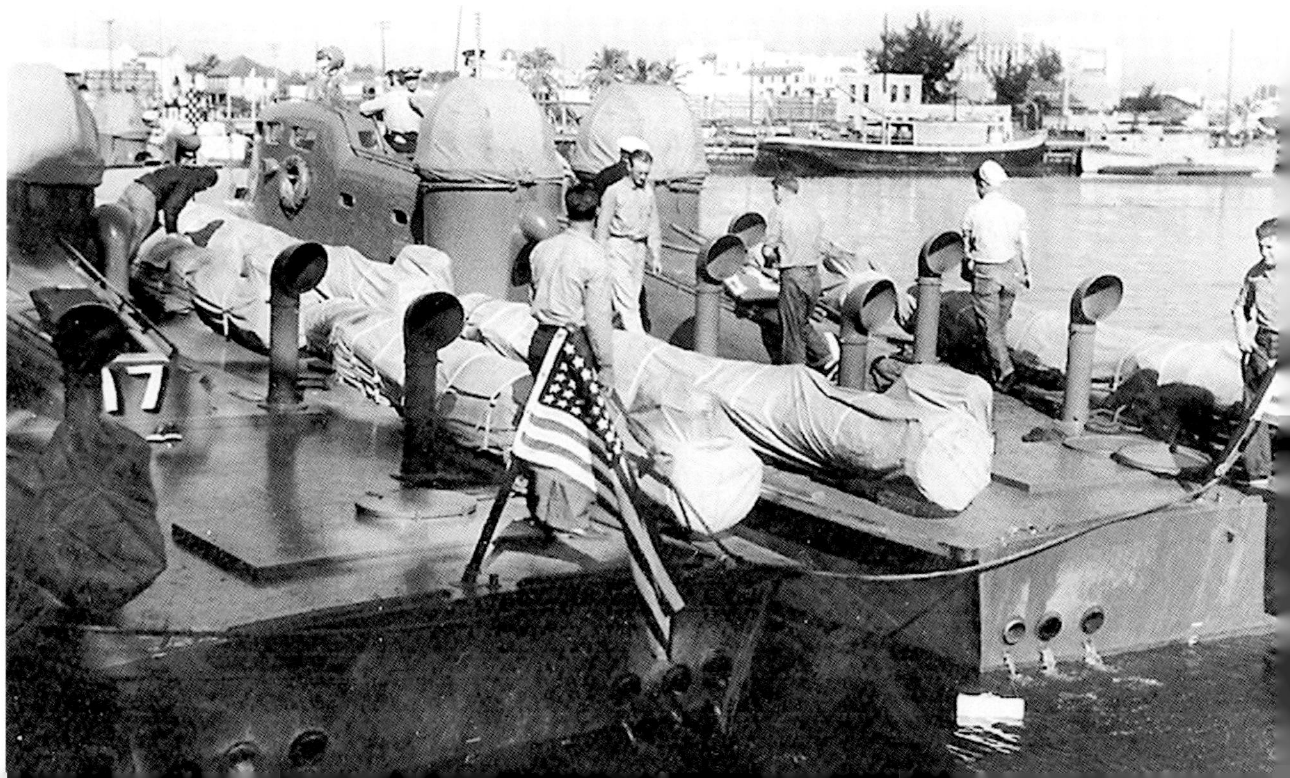

This is a photo of Elco 70 footers PT17 and PT18 at Miami, Florida. *Courtesy of Frank Andruss*

The turrets are PT17 on her way from Key West to New York, March 1941. *Courtesy of Frank Andruss & John C. Kenney*

Pictured are crew members on the bridge of PT15 in Cuba. Note the sleek line of the boat and a good shot of the life saver. *Courtesy of Frank Andruss*

This photo was taken from the Elco 70 footer to show the USS *Niagara* AGP-1 tender in the background. *Courtesy of Frank Andruss & John C. Kenney*

This is a photo of an Elco 70 footer listing to starboard in Cuba.
Courtesy of Frank Andruss

PV-70, the Elco purchased Scott-Paine boat, out of the water.
Courtesy of Elco

Taboga Island, Panama, was an operational training base in August 1942. Squadrons bound for the Pacific Theater passed through this base, where refitting was done on some boats. The base closed in March 1946. *Courtesy of the PT Boat Museum*

Elco 77s moored to the pier during commissioning ceremonies at the base at Taboga Island, just off the Pacific entrance to the Panama Canal. Some of these boats were incorrectly numbered to confuse the "enemy." The correct numbers were 46, 40, 61, 48, and 45 read from the nearest boat to the back. *Courtesy of Frank Andruss*

This is a photo of PT47 being off loaded at Panama.
Courtesy of the National Archives

PT 10 on measured miles off the Elco plant at Bayonne, NJ.

This is a photo of PT17 on maneuvers off Miami, February 1941. *Courtesy of Elco*

PT19, replica of the Scott-Paine model, was transferred to the British under lend-lease in July 1941. *Courtesy of Ted Walther*

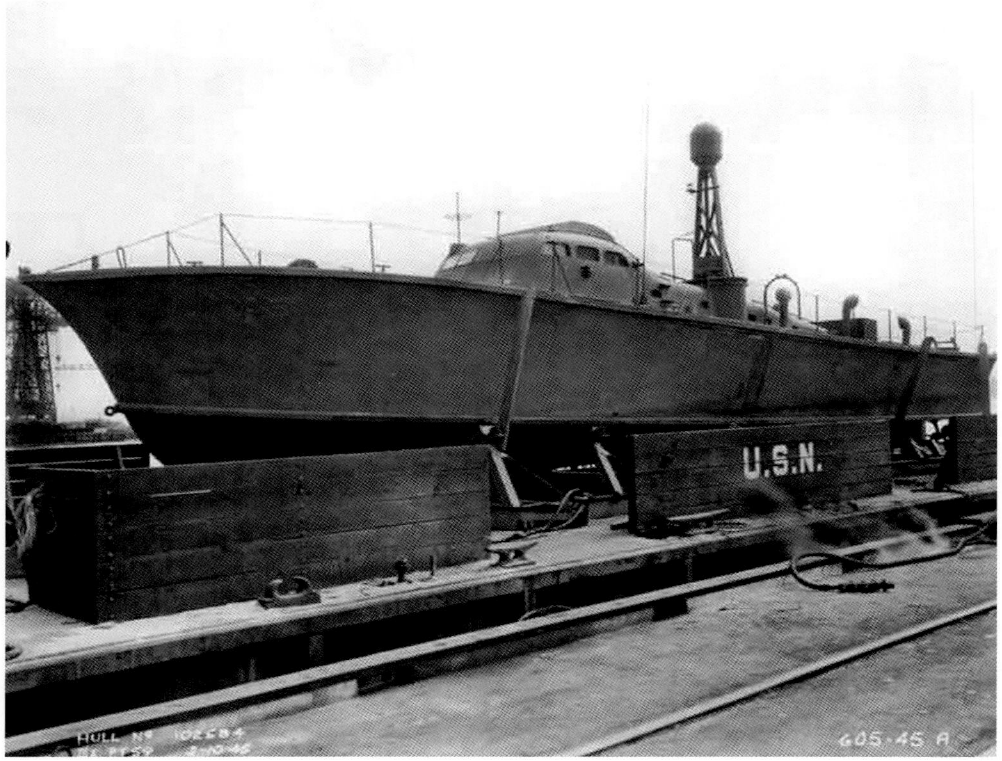

PT 59 shows the towing eye attached to the bow below deck, just where the chine rails meet. It was used for towing the boat in calm water. *Courtesy of the PT Boat Museum*

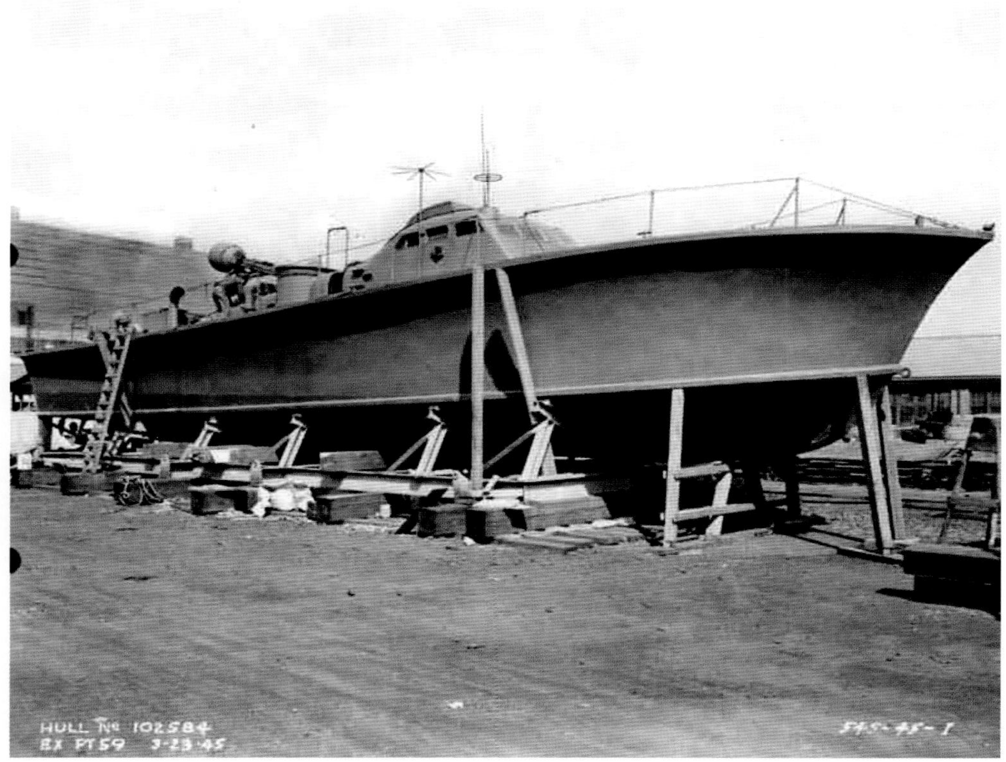

Above and next page: an Elco 77' PT boat near completion. *Courtesy of National Archives*

Elco 77' running in formation off the East Coast. *Courtesy of Elco*

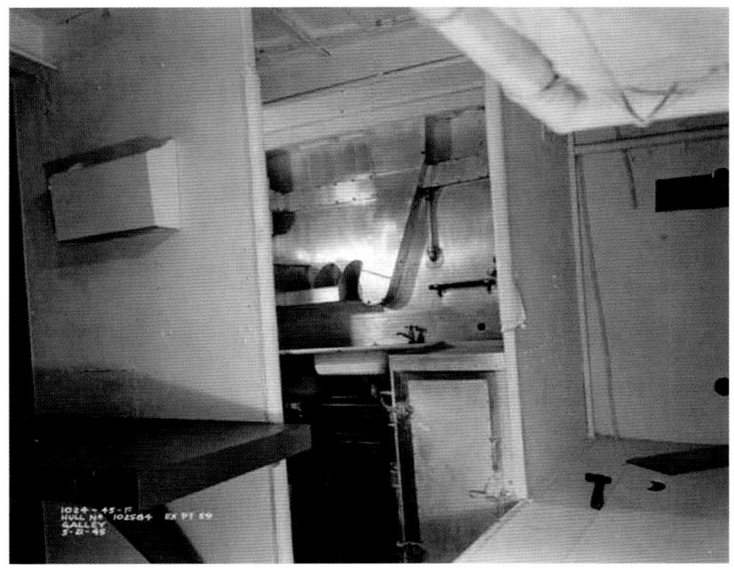

Above and following: photos of the interior of a 77' Elco. *Courtesy of the National Archives*

ENGINE ROOM
5-21-45

HULL No 102584
545-45-E

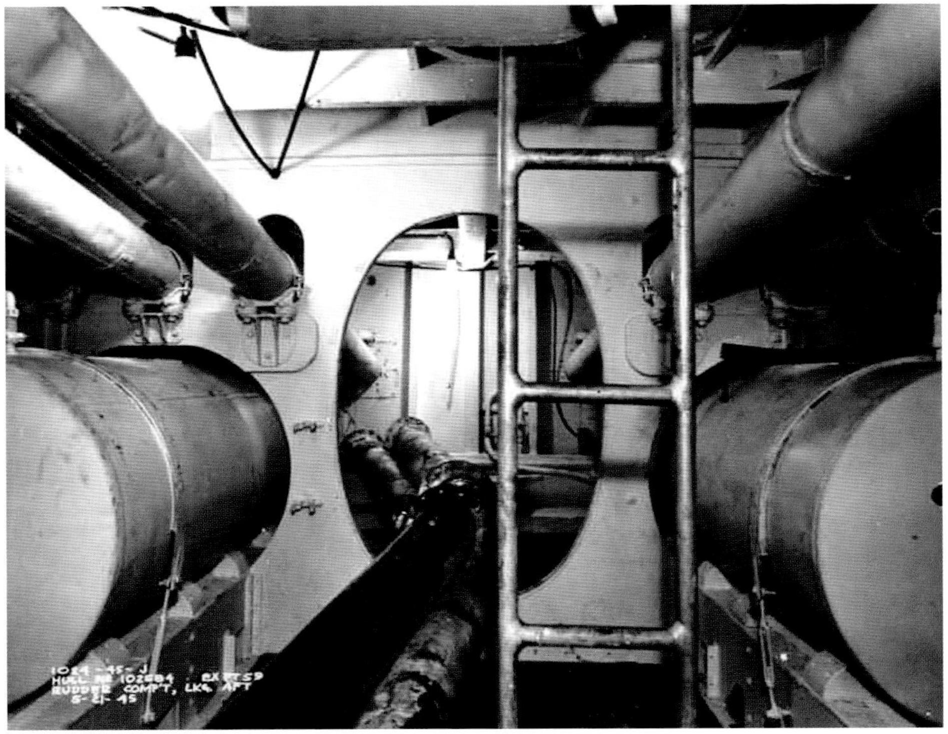
1024-45-J
COMPT, LKG. AFT
5-21-45

Pictured is PT103, Elco's first 80' boat, getting ready for time trails. On the bridge is Irwin Chase, Sr., second from the left, naval architect and chief designer; Henry R. Sutphen, Executive Vice President, fourth from the left; and Preston Sutphen, General Manager, back row in the light suit. *Courtesy of Elco*

Pictured is PT103 idling away from the Elco dock shortly after its launching, May 16, 1942. Ens. Richard E. Keresey, future CO of PT105, is at the wheel. Note the absence of mufflers. *Courtesy of the National Archives*

This photo is PT48, taken July 3, 1942, off Toboga Island, Panama Canal Zone. *Courtesy of the US Navy*

PT107 - 110 secured aboard Liberty ship SS *Joseph Standon* prior to transport to Panama. *Courtesy of US Navy*

Ron 5's PT 103, an 80 foot Elco, refueling from the seaplane tender USS *Pocomoke* near the Galapagos Islands in 1942. PT 103 was put in service in June 1942 and was transferred to Ron 18 in February 1945.

The bow view of the Elco 77 footer clearly shows the unique slanting of the deck that is typical for this type of boat. *Courtesy of the National Archives*

Pictured is Irwin Chase (1883-1974) with scarf. Chase was a graduate of the University of Michigan with a degree in Marine Engineering. He was Elco's chief designer from 1906 to 1923, and then served as Elco general manager before retiring in 1949. He was often mistakenly credited with earning a Silver Star during World War II. In fact, it was his son, Rear Admiral Irwin "Mike" Chase, who received this award. *Courtesy of the PT Boat Museum*

8

Cockpit

This image is the cockpit of PV-70, which became PT9. *Courtesy of Frank A. Andruss*

The two "sights" on top of the cockpit are for the two 5" rocket launchers mounted on the foredeck. *Courtesy of William Maloney via Jerry Gilmartin*

This is a picture of the Elco 80' cockpit. Note the torpedo director at the extreme upper right of the picture. The device to the right of the clock is a standard Pelorus for shooting bearings; not standard equipment. The small lever on the side of the throttle control is a ratchet handle that, when tightened, put tension on the throttle levers to lock the throttles at the desired speed. When it is loosened free movement is resumed. *Courtesy of Charlie Jones*

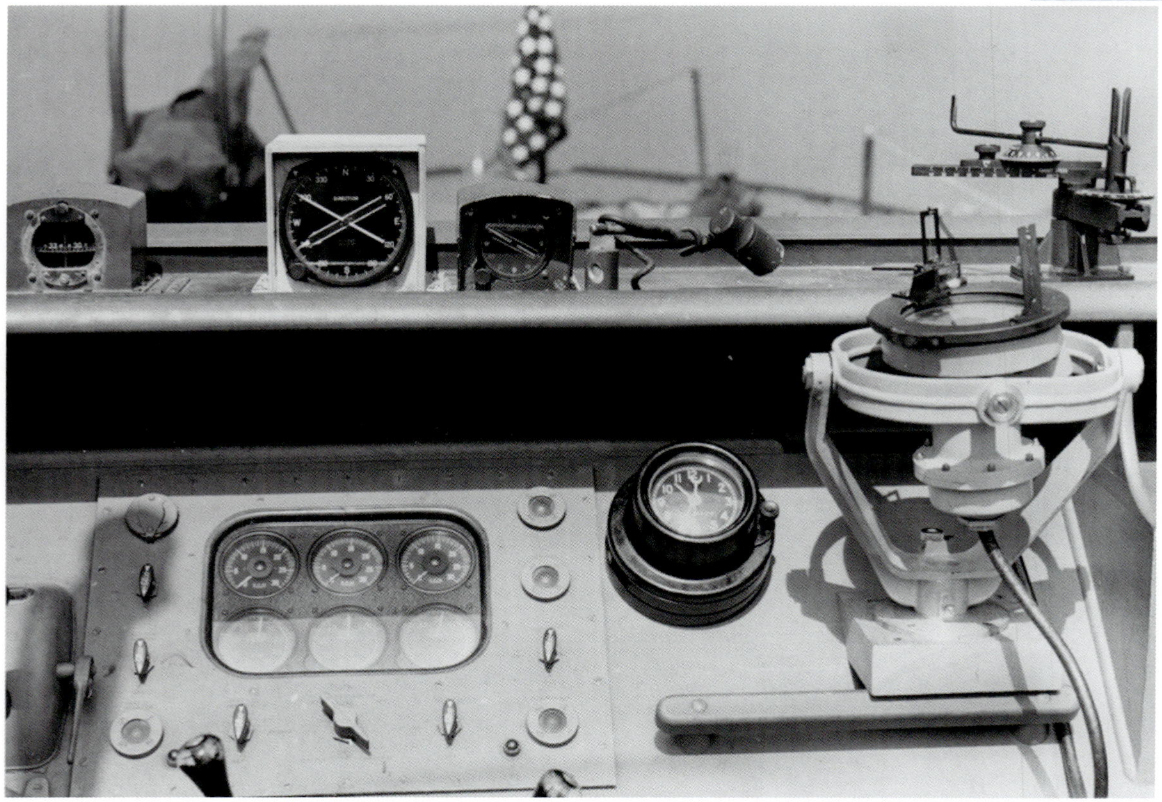

This is a close up shot of Higgins PT461. There is also an aluminum binnacle that holds a Mark 8 aircraft magnetic compass. You can also see the fluxgate compass slave indicator next to the binnacle. At the center of the windscreen is a pedestal mount surface for the torpedo aiming device, which is not mounted. *Courtesy of Jerry Gilmartin*

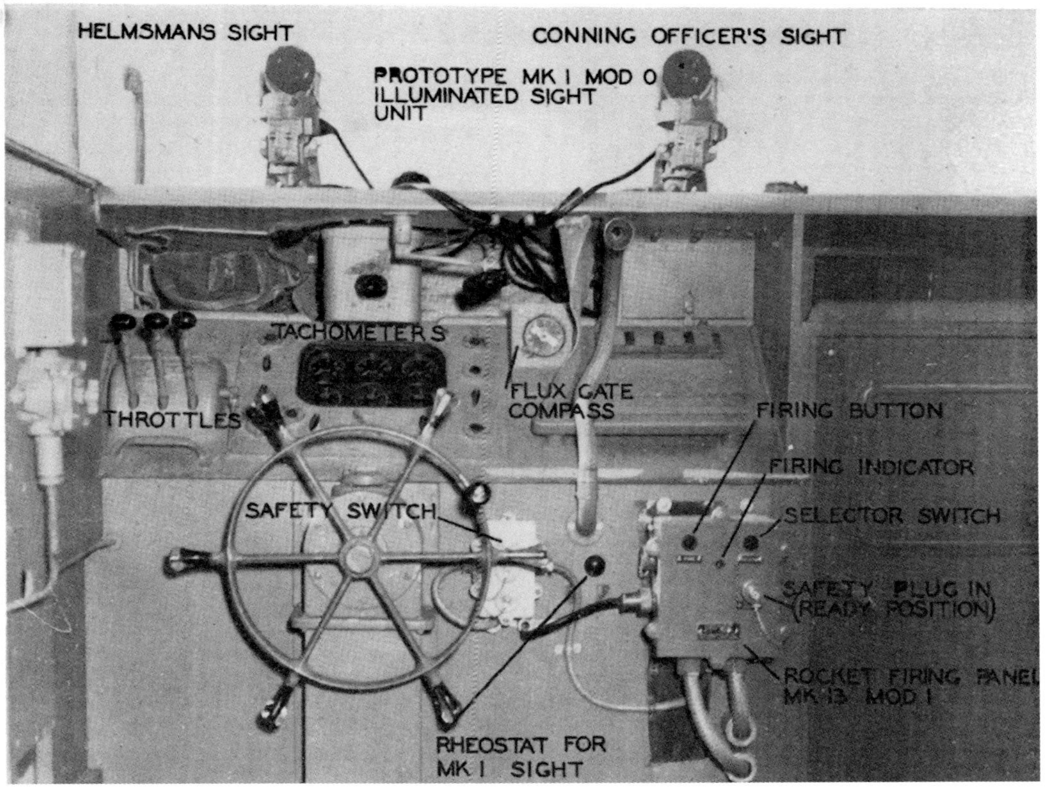

Cockpit of PT 557. The sights on top are for an MK 50 5 inch rocket launcher. *Courtesy of Al Ross*

9

Elcoplane

The PT boat made by Elco was a planing hull type. The hydrodynamic forces lift the hull out of the water, thus reducing drag and allowing more speed. The stepped hull design can maintain near optimum trim across a wider planing speed envelope, and the amount of wetted area is reduced, resulting in less drag and obtaining higher speeds. Multiple steps were an attempt to get the benefit of the step hull, maximize stability, and make the hull more sea worthy.

The function of the louvers on the sides of the boat are to provide air that exits through the vent at the rear face of the steps under the boat. This creates a layer of air under the hull for the boat to ride, thus resulting in fewer drags. This allows the boat to obtain more speed.

In December 1943 six special steps, or Elcoplanes, were fitted to the bottom of PT487. The boat was equipped with three Packard W-14 marine engines. On a light displacement of 90,300, PT487 hit 55.95 knots during trials for the Board of Inspection & Survey and made a 180 degree turn at top speed in six seconds. The Board was impressed by the performance and recommended to incorporate them in the regular production of boat builders. BuShip even planned to send kits to the field to convert the operating boats. Then PT560 through 563 of Squadron 29, equipped with Elcoplanes, ran more tests on a trip from New York to Miami. It was on this long cruise that the faults showed up. At cruising speeds the boats burned 25% more fuel and 75% more lube oil. Steering was more difficult and acceleration dropped off, and the boats tended to root into heavy seas. The tests also showed that at speeds below 2200 rpm, the standard boat was superior to the Elcoplane boat in maneuvering and steering. After considering the results, the Bureau decided to abandon the project. However, in special high speed operation an Elcoplane installation would have been a valuable addition.

The ELCOplane Design

By the end of 1942 PT boat officers were requesting major changes to the boats based on the combat experiences in the Philippines and at Guadalcanal. The most urgent need was for faster craft as the boats where barely able to outrun Japanese destroyers. The perceived need for additional speed drove the builders to enhance the design of their PT boat craft. While Higgins designed an entirely new boat, the Hellcat, to address this need Irwin Chase and his design team were pressured by ELCO management to focus on a modification to the 80 foot design then in production. Improved designs to produce additional speed had to be incorporated in the standard eighty foot hull to avoid any production delays associated with shifting to construction of a new hull design. Chase started work in 1943 to incorporate technology that he had developed in 1911 for a high speed hydroplaning hull that would ultimately be referred to as the ELCOplane.

Patented in 1913, the ELCOplane concept created a true hydroplane. Chase's design concept was ingenious and simple. By attaching a lateral series of six simple wedge shaped steps to the hull bottom and seventh trim plate step to the stern (see drawings) Chase converted a planing hull to a hydroplane. The principle of the multiple steps was: to cut down on wetted surfaces, break suction under the after body and to increase lift. (Lord, 1963) Since each of these steps was of a much higher aspect ratio than the hull as a whole the full weight of the boat could be supported on these seven thin steps, rather than on the complete planing surface of the standard eighty foot ELCO boat. The steps were designed to introduce air into the flow to reduce wetted surface and the drag associated with the contact with the water. The stepped hull not only reduced the drag on the boat's hull, but at the same time enhanced the lift production, resulting in the hull riding higher out of the water. These effects provided dramatically increased speed for the same amount of engine power. This point was proven out by the ELCOplane trials performed with PT-487 by the Board of Inspection & Survey in December 1943. The PT-487 equipped with standard Packard W-14 engines at war load [109,300 lbs] and light load [90,300 lbs] PT-487 operated at speeds of 53.62 knots and 55.95 knots respectively. This represented a ten-knot improvement of speed of over that of the standard production boat.

Chase further enhanced the step design by hastening the elimination of suction under the hull by adding air ducts to the side of the boat, introducing air above the chine of the boat. (Chase, 1913) These air vents are called louvers in most discussions of the ELCOplane. The vacuum under the hull created by the water flow over the foils sucked air through the louvers into the voids, breaking the suction and allowing the boat to skim the surface on the steps. The louvers pointed towards the stern, presumably to exclude spray and get only air into the area behind each step.

The Bureau of Ships was so impressed with the performance of the ELCOPlane that four boats of Squadron 29, PTs 560 through 563, where equipped with the hull enhancement. Orders were issued to change all new construction contracts to the ELCOPlane while retrofit kits were ordered for boats already in the field. While these production plans were being made Squadron 29 embarked on a shakedown cruise from New York City to Miami. During this cruise the ELCOPlane exhibited a number of problems: excessive lubrication oil consumption (attributed to improper design of water intakes), and damaged louvers. These problems could have been overcome by design changes. However, the boat captains stated the boats were sensitive to trim, weight distribution on the boat. From their perspective this senstivitiy was inducing handeling difficulties with the ELCOplane equiped boats. (Bennett & Tredinnick, 1947) Most likely these difficulties were due to the ELCOplane changing the center of lift of the boat. Indeed Chase's design had a fundemental flaw, improper location of the center of gravity of the boat with respect to its new center of lift. A proper design of the ELCOplane would have required changes in the weight distribution of the boat. To accomplish this large internal changes to the design of the boat, such as moving the engine room forward in the hull, would have been required. The ultimate demise of the ELCOplane was this misplaced weight distribution within the hull of a standard 80 foot ELCO PT boat. Without a major redesign of the boat's arrangement the ELCOplane was a design that led to poor handling characteristics.

PT Boat Hydrodynamics

Basics of a Planing Hull Design

Motor Torpedo Boats were designed to fly, fly on the surface of the water in a physical phenomenon called planing. The physics of planing are very similar to the physics of an airplane flying in the air. Airplanes fly by creating lift over a wing when the wing is pushed with sufficient speed through the air. PT boats generate lift by moving a flat surface in the water at sufficient speed, a process not unlike skipping a flat stone over the surface of a lake.

Those familiar with aerodynamics understand that airplanes are immersed in a fluid, air. An airplane's wing is shaped to rotate the air passing over it downward. This creates a circulation (rotational flow) of the air flowing past the wing. The combination of this rotation and the free air stream results in higher flow speeds on top of the wing than under it. A pressure difference occurs with the air on the bottom side of the wing being higher than that on the upper side of the wing. The higher pressure air literally pushes the wing up into the lower pressure air on the upper portion of the wing. If this lift force is high enough the plane flies. PT boats are similar but a little different in that the lift surface, the bottom of the hull, is intended to ride on the top of their fluid media, water. When a properly shaped planing boat moves faster across the water, it pushes some of the water downward, because of the shape of the hull and its running trim angle. This downward change in speed (momentum) of the water creates an equal and opposite reaction that appears as a lifting force applied to the hull. However, the lift created by a planing hull is much less efficient than the lift created by an airplane wing, because there is no upper surface to experience a suction force, and also because the aspect ratio is much different (lower for the planing boat). The *aspect ratio* is defined as the square of the span, divided by the area of an airfoil or wing. The span is the length perpendicular to the flow and the area is the projected or planform area, viewed from above. In the case of an aircraft, a wing can readily be made eight or ten times as wide as it is long. The aspect ratio is related to efficiency at lift production because the high pressure fluid under the wing (or hull) is trying to fill the vacuum on top of it. High aspect makes it easier to seal off the two areas from each other, leading to a bigger pressure differential. However a boat needs to be longer than it is wide to reach speeds to get over the hump and into a planing mode. This creates an inherent design conflict with boats, the need for a long hull to reach planing speed conflicts with the need for a large aspect ratio for efficient planing. The other difference between planing craft and airplanes are the resistive forces. (du Cane, 1956)

To state the obvious, water has different properties than that of air. Water is much more viscous than air, and also approximately 800 times as dense as air. A relatively small planform area, relative to the wing area required for an airplane, will be sufficient to make a boat "fly". However a boat loses about half its lift through not having an upper surface that's "wetted." The viscosity, as well as the higher density, of water creates much higher frictional drag forces than are experienced in air. A boat's drag can be seen as of two kinds: a tangential shear force along the hull surface from the internal friction or viscosity of the water, and a pressure force, perpendicular to the hull surface, resulting from the hull's pushing water aside as it moves ahead. This pressure force is mainly a wave drag force that is related to the length of the boat. A boat's wave drag peaks at a speed in knots of 1.34 times the square root of the waterline length in feet. (For an 80 foot PT boat this works out to approximately 12 knots). This is informally called the "hull speed" of the boat, to get up on plane it is necessary for the boat's propulsion equipment to push the boat through the large bow-wave that will build up at hull speed. Both of these forces combine to inhibit the ability of a boat to reach a plane, get over the hump. Getting over the hump takes power, power to overcome the drag effects that inhibit planing and to achieve the speeds necessary to generate enough lift forces to cause the boat to start rising up out of the water. Once achieved, the lifting force mentioned earlier results in planing; facilitating a dramatically reduced wetted surface area providing less frictional drag. The wave drag also decreases, because there is less immersed volume than is required to hold up the boat's weight, and therefore less water needs to be pushed aside by the advancing boat. (Lord, 1963)

American PT Boat Hull Forms

The most efficient shape for planing is an infinitely wide flat plate, which has an infinite aspect ratio. This is not to say that planing cannot be induced in a rounded hull. The Germans were very successful in accomplishing this with their Schnellboote designs. However British and American designers tended to move towards the flat plate design utilizing a hard chine. A hard chine hull is more efficient because water flow moves aft and outboard from the keel line as the boat advances in the typical planing attitude of about 3 degrees bow up. When the water reached the hard chine it just kept on going outboard in a sheet of spray, while a round bilge hull tends to climb up the topsides, resulting in additional wetted surface frictional drag.

The American boats manufacturers, ELCO, Higgins and Huckins all came up with slightly different hull designs using a hard chine to create as flat a plate as possible in the stern. To complicate the design challenge flat plates cannot accommodate wave action. Flat plates creating pounding forces on waves that ultimately can destroy the structure of the boat. Flat plates also do not provide any assistance with direction control, they tend to yaw, or skate of the surface of the water. The design solution for all three American PT boat manufacturers was a sharp V shape hull at the stem lofting towards the stern to a fairly narrow V (a flat plane), the minimum necessary to provide assistance with directional control. (Lord, 1963) The "deadrise angle", the angle between the V-shaped section of the boat and a horizontal line through the keel, was an important design element in any V-bottomed planing boat. Angles of 20 degrees result in a smooth ride but less efficiency, because the lift force is not directed straight up from each half of the boat, but some of it is wasted by pressing the halves of the hull together; also, the "deep-V" hull has more wetted surface. Small deadrise angles, under 10 degrees, result in violent pounding but the boat will have more lift and less drag. Normally the deadrise angle is measured at the stern, because that part of the boat is always immersed, while most of the bow and often part of the midships area comes out of water at extreme speeds.

The best hull form

For years the subject of which PT boat was better has been debated by those who rode the boats. Lindsay Lord, the designer of the Huckins boat, sheds light on the subject. The evaluation of the hull design is fairly involved mathematical analysis of the geometry. In summary a boat that best emulates a flat plane over the entire lifting surface will provide the best performance. Indeed the Higgins PT boat carried the loft of the V further towards the stern (into the lifting wetted surface) leading to more friction drag and less lift which inhibit the speed of the boat. However this same V provided better directional control at speed than that of the ELCO design, which did not carry as deep of a V into the wetted planing area. Hence the ELCO was a faster boat (less drag forces) but lacked the maneuverability of the Higgins boat. Huckins provided the most efficient hull, providing the flattest surface across the width of the hull from the beginning of the lifting surface. Direction control was enabled by including a keel skeg (exposed keel) along most of the length of the hull. As no controlled tests of the Huckins boats related to the ELCO and Higgins boats were ever carried out, it is hard to tell if the Huckins design was superior in performance. However the skeg presented a design feature that slowed the construction of the boats as well as added cost. (Lord, 1963) .

Bibliography

Bennett, H. L., & Tredinnick, F. A. (1947). *An Administrative History of PT Boats in World War II.* Washington D.C.: United States Department of the Navy.

Du Cane, P. (1956). *High-Speed Small Craft.* London: Purnell and Sons, Limited.

Chase, I. (1913). *Patent No. 1050517.* USA.

Lord, L. (1963). *Naval Architecture of Planing Hulls.* Cambridge, MD: Cornell Maritime Press, Inc.

PT 487, one of five boats equipped with Elcoplane, underway for a test run. The louvers on the side of the boat had not been installed yet. *Courtesy of PT Boat Museum*

Chalk mark "PT 562," barely visible on the cradle, indicates this is PT 562, one of four boats of Ron 29 equipped with the Elcoplane System. The six louvers on each side of the boat were part of the system. The six steps attached to the bottom of the hull can barely be seen. *Courtesy of the PT Boat Museum*

This is PT 487, even though the cradle was marked PT 562. Note the number 487 barely visible on the engine room hatch. At this angle the openings of all six louvers can be seen clearly. The steps are visible just under the chine. Note the last step extended 17 inches beyond the stern of the boat. *Courtesy of the PT Boat Museum*

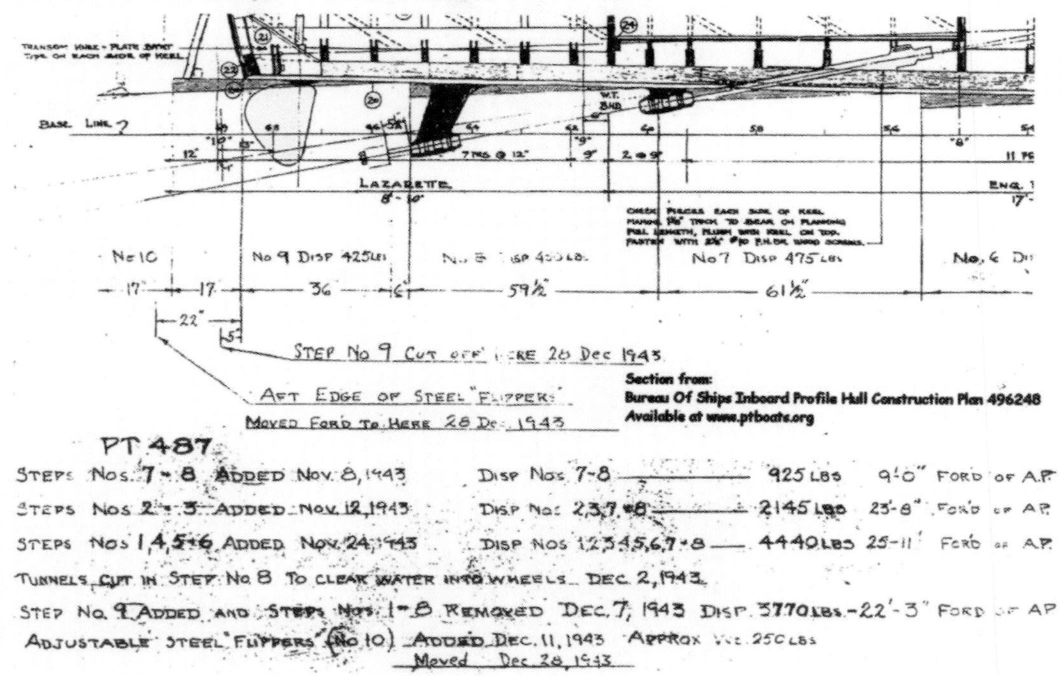

This is PT 487, even though the cradle was marked PT 562.

10

PTC

Motor Boat Submarine Chaser Squadron 1 consisted of PTC-1 to PTC-12. John D. Bulkeley was the commander from February 10 to July 17, 1941. The boats were modified 70' Elco PT boats. They carried 24 depth charges, stern ash can racks, and two Y-guns able to throw two charges from each side simultaneously. They were also equipped with different types of sound gears. In the summer of 1941 they went to Key West, Florida, for testing. The result was disappointing because the sound gears were unable to locate the submarine due to the loud Packard engines drowning out the echoes. The boats returned to New York. They were then transferred to the British in April 1941 under lend-lease for conversion to motor gun boats (MGB).

PTC-12 showing its depth charge transfer racks. *Courtesy of the PT Boat Museum*

PTC showing its depth charge equipment and arbor stowage.

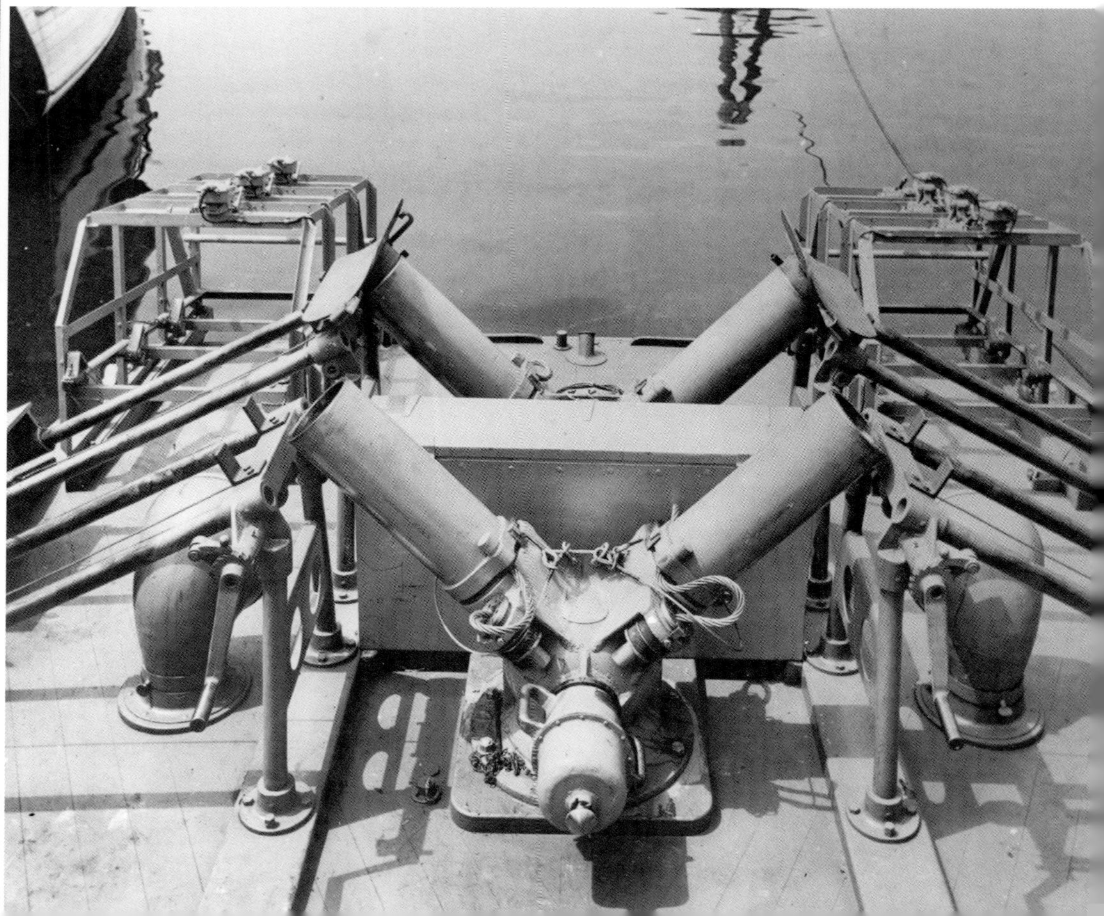

The PTC after deck showing its Y-guns and depth charge dropping racks.

11

Higgins

Higgins Industries' $5 million plant facilities that employed 13,000 men and women. *Courtesy of Higgins Industries*

The original Higgins Industries complex was located on the Industrial Canal, July 1942. *Courtesy of Howard Hollem via Ferg*

Andrew Jackson Higgins (August 28, 1886 - August 1, 1952) was the founder and owner of Higgins Industries, the New Orleans based manufacturer of PT boats. In addition to building PT boats, he also designed and built landing craft.

The Higgins 70-footer, called the Hellcat, is being hoisted to Lake Pontchartrain for test run. It could make a top speed of 46 knots. The Navy gave it number PT564. *Courtesy of the Library of Congress*

This photo is a Hellcat getting ready for a trial run. *Courtesy of Higgins*

Hellcat plaque. *Courtesy of Charlie Jones*

Special fixed .50 cal. machine guns aboard a Higgins Hellcat at the training center in Miami, Florida.

Pictured is a 70' MRB built by Higgins for the Royal Northland Navy. *Courtesy of Al Ross*

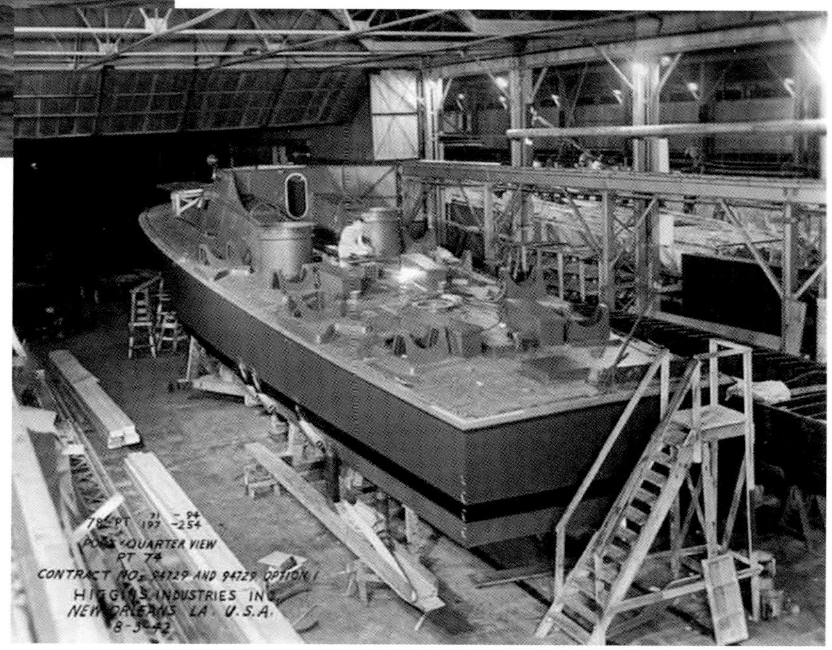

Pictured is PT74 under construction, port quarter view. *Courtesy of Higgins Industries*

This is a photo of the port quarter view of PT75 and PT76 under construction. *Courtesy of National Archives*

Pictured are the different stages of construction. *Courtesy of Higgins Industries*

This is a photo of the Higgins 78' PT78 ready for a test run. *Courtesy of Higgins Industries*

Higgins PT80 undergoing a test run before being turned over to the Navy. *Courtesy of Higgins Industries*

Pictured is a PT87 waiting to be launched into the water. *Courtesy of Higgins Industries*

Pictured is PT325 underway during a test run. *Courtesy of the US Navy*

Pictured is PT296 in New Orleans Lake. It was placed in service October 18, 1943, then transferred to Ron 4 on 4 December. *Courtesy of Higgins Industries*

Unidentified Higgins boats maneuver, April 20, 1944. *Courtesy of PT Boat Museum*

PTs 627 (left) and 628 were transferred to the USSR. *Courtesy of PT Boat Museum*

Rare picture of a Higgins boat tied to a tender to refuel in 1945. *Courtesy of Scott Cunningham*

The last US Navy Higgins PT boat converted to a target boat. This craft was assigned to the Surface Craft Division at Port Hueneme, California. *Courtesy of Victor Chun*

Higgins boats in formation.

Higgins PT 297. *Courtesy of the PT Boat Museum*

This is an unusual view of a Higgins boat.

Pictured is PT 227's engine room. *Courtesy of the PT Boat Museum*

Ron 43, PT 632 with PT 625 in front, on board transport for transfer to the USSR.
Courtesy of the PT Boat Museum

Higgins PT 295 Cockpit. *Courtesy of Frank Andruss*

Higgins boats bound for the USSR. *Courtesy of the PT Boat Museum*

12

Melville
The Motor Torpedo Boat Squadrons Training Center

The Motor Torpedo Boat Squadrons Training Center (MTBSTC) was established on February 17, 1942, by the order of the Secretary of the Navy. Led by Lieutenant Commander William C. Specht, USN, known as "Spect Tech," the Center began its operations with ten boats of MTB Squadron Four (Elco 77 footers PTs 59-68).

By April 1942, there were 51 officers and 177 enlisted men learning the rudimentary skills of PT boat operation. 47 Quonset huts were in various stages of completion, and 44 more huts were requested to be built. Eventually the Center would have 13 buildings for office space, 35 classrooms, 42 maintenance buildings, and 197 huts for living quarters. This allowed the Center to host 90 officers and 860 sailors in a three month training period. By March 1945, the Center had trained 1,797 officers and 11,668 blue jackets.

Commander Thomas G. Warfield. C.O. MTB Training Base, Melville, RI. He de-commissioned the base on November 1945. A total of 12,500 enlisted men and 2,017 officers were indoctrinated in PT boat operations. *Courtesy of Arthur Barnes*

This is a forward view of PT61's cabin while idling out on a training cruise. *Courtesy of the National Archives*

John F. Kennedy

possibly Hamlin D. Smith

Pictured is JFK's class at Melville, RI.

.50 caliber lecture on PT66. *Courtesy of the National Archives*

The second Melville officer's training class, July 1942. Many would go to Squadrons Five and Six; a few would face the Tokyo Express in the Solomons. *Courtesy of George Brooks*

This is a photo of PT boat officers undergoing training on board PT66. *Courtesy of the National Archives*

Officers at the MTBSTC learned how to operate the .50 cal. machine gun turrets.
Courtesy of Frank Andruss

Aerial view of PT 487 underway at Melville, RI.
Courtesy of the PT Boat Museum

The boat at the center is PT545, taken February 1945 at the Finger Pier at Melville. *Courtesy of Frank Andruss*

This is a rare look at firing a practice torpedo in the bay at Melville. *Courtesy of Frank Andruss*

Pictured is a PT40 and a 77 footer arriving at Melville. All these 77 footers were assigned to MTBRTU to use in hull repair training. *Courtesy of Frank Andruss*

This is a 77 footer that was cannibalized and sitting in its cradle. Notice the Ball Field near the water's edge. *Courtesy of Frank Andruss*

Pictured is a 77 footer at Melville using the crane to move the Cabin Trunk. *Courtesy of Frank Andruss*

This is PT317 in January 1945; a layer of ice covered the boat. *Courtesy of Frank Andruss*

This is PT534 returning from training and entering Cove to the finger Piers.
Courtesy of Frank Andruss

Aerial view of two Elco boats on a training mission at Melville, RI.
Courtesy of the PT Boat Museum

PTs 138 and 140 at dock at Melville, RI. *Courtesy of Charles S. Haynsworth*

PT315 (left) and PT139 pointed out and ready for training. *Courtesy of Frank Andruss*

Pictured is PT139 at the dock.
Courtesy of Frank Andruss

Both boats carry no torpedoes.

Ron 29 taken at Melville. *Courtesy of Frank Andruss*

PT 613 was transferred to the Operational Development Force, the last PTs remaining in service. *Courtesy of the PT Boat Museum*

PT 98 Crew (Ron 14) and Mrs. Roosevelt, the First Lady. The crew had given her a ride on their PT boat.

Training gears and torpedo tubes litter the ground at the edge of the water.
Courtesy of Frank Andruss

80 foot Elco iced in at Melville, January 15, 1945.

After the graduation from MTBSTC at Melville, RI, the next proud moment is Ron 27 being commissioned at the New York Naval Shipyard.

Ron 40 being commissioned at the New York Naval Shipyard under the command of LT Commander George E. Cox, Jr. *Courtesy of the National Archives*

13

Torpedo Tubes

The torpedo tubes for the Elco and Higgins were of different design. The Elco used black powder charged tubes which utilized an impulse cartridge inserted into the firing mechanism. Higgins used compressed air to propel the torpedoes, with a compressor to refill the impulse chamber to fire the torpedoes. Those Elco boats exported to the Soviets were converted to the compressed air tubes to operate better in extreme cold. For this reason, almost all the boats that participated in the Aleutian campaign were Higgins boats. The original torpedo tube for the Higgins boat had the curved air impulse chamber designated the 21 inch Mark 19 Mod 4. It was mounted on top of the tube. The other type of tube was designed for the later Mark 13 torpedo and had two straight parallel air chambers mounted side by side on top of the tube.

The original torpedo tube for the Higgins boat had the curved air impulse chamber designated the 21 inch Mark 19 Mod 4. It was mounted on top of the tube. The other type of tube designed for the later Mark 13 torpedo had two straight parallel air chambers mounted beside one another on the top of the tube.

Close-up view of an Elco 80 foot PT boat torpedo tube with the cap on. *Courtesy of Elco*

Ron 15 boats at Sardinia. Note the compressed air torpedo tubes on the Higgins boats.
Courtesy of the National Archives

Ron 15 Higgins boats at Sarnia show the port side of the torpedo tubes.
Courtesy of the National Archives

Mark 8, 21 inch torpedo being loaded into its tube aboard PT21. *Courtesy of the National Archives*

14

Camouflage

The USN used the colors in the 1929 Munsell Book of Color for WWII paints. However, in 1944 Munsell started revising their color notation system, and there is no correlation between the color notations in the current book and the original 1929 edition. This makes it difficult for modelers today to mix paint to match the exact color unless a 1929 Munsell Book of Color is available. Since Federal Standard (FS) no. 595 with paint chips can still be obtained, most modelers use the FS numbers as reference, as in this book. In general, PT boat camouflage is divided into two types: Concealment is used to blend with the background and surroundings, while Confusion provides a patterned paint scheme to confuse the enemy.

This table represents the WWII Navy color designations to match the Federal Standard (FS) chips which can still be obtained from the General Services Administration, Washington, DC.

Factory painted Ron 10 PT 166, 1942. *Courtesy of Ted Walther*

Color Name	Color Designation	FS 595 Number
Light Grey	5-L	36440
		36492
Ocean Grey	5-O	36176
Pale Grey	5-P	36586
Haze Grey	5-H	36306
Dark Grey	5-D	35526
Green 1 (haze green)	5HG	34373
Green 2 (ocean green)	5-OG	34227
Green 3 (navy green)	5NG	34128
Deck Green	2OG	34092
Navy Blue	5-N	25053
White	5-U	37875
Black	82	37038
Copperoyd		30109
Deck Blue	20B	35164

Measure is the system the US Navy used to designate 33 patents and designs of paint schemes for ships and boats.

Measure 1	
Dark Grey	5-D
Measure 13	
Haze Grey	5-H
Measure 14	
Ocean Grey	5-O
Measure 31	
Black	82
Ocean Green	5-OG
Navy Green	5-NG

The above measures were used for PT boats during WWII.

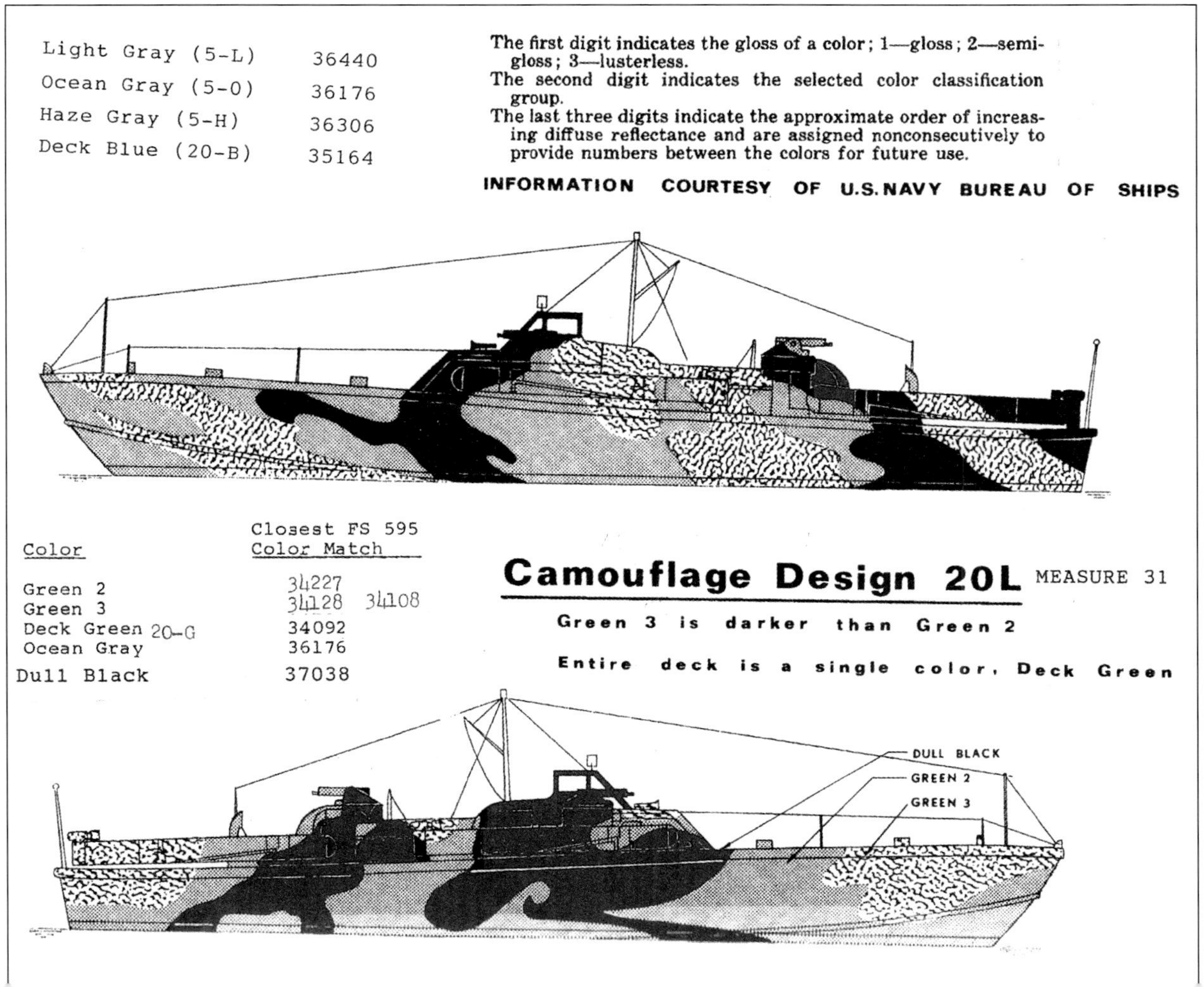

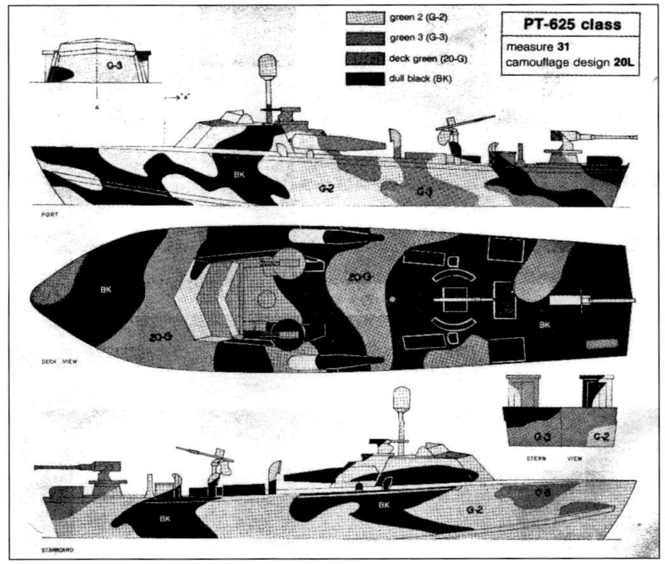

A camouflage net rests on PT 351. *Courtesy of the PT Boat Museum*

15

Armaments

This is a close-up view of the Dewendre turret on an early Elco 77' boat. *Courtesy of Elco*

This photo, dated 1942, was taken at Pearl City Yacht Club. *Courtesy of Jerry Gilmartin*

PT156 in Tulagi, June 1944, refitted with a MK-12 20 mm Scarf Ring mount in the forward starboard turret, which was developed and manufactured at the New York Navy Yard for PTs in 1942. *Courtesy of Wayne Traxel*

PT157 refitted with MK 12 20 mm mounted in the forward starboard turret.

Another view of the loaded Thunderbolt. *Courtesy of Elco*

Thunderbolt, one of the first prototypes and installed on PT 138, was ripped from its foundation on the deck and lost in heavy seas. Improved models were installed on four boats of Ron 29 (PT556 - 559) in 1944 and on a few boats of Ron 10 and 21 in 1945 in the Philippines. They were highly satisfactory during their few actions. *Courtesy of Elco*

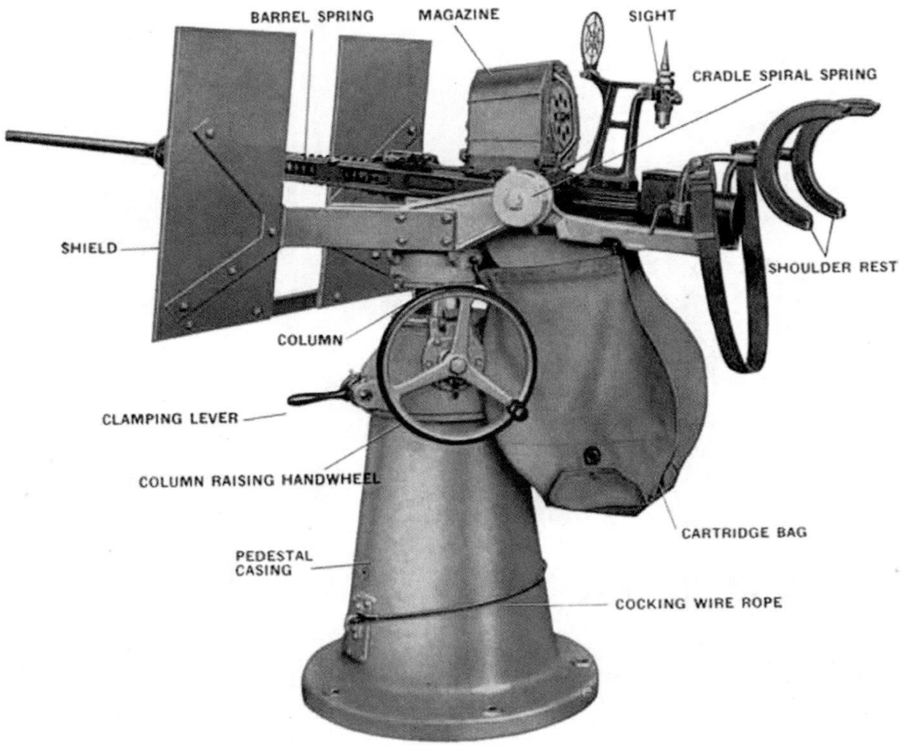

20 MM Antiaircraft Gun

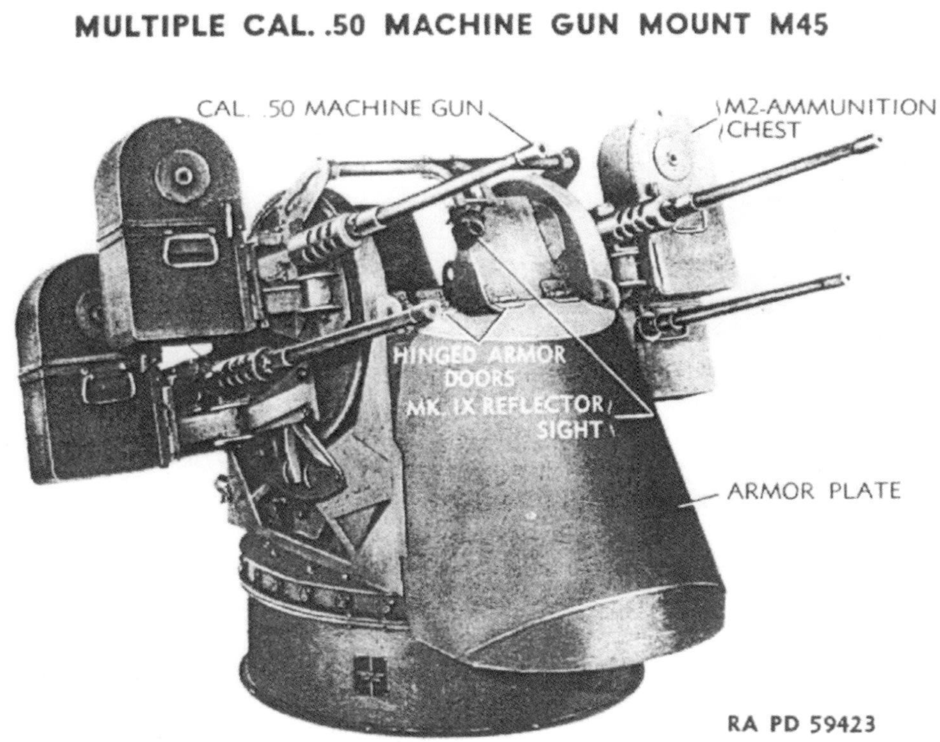

Figure 2—Multiple Cal. .50 Machine Gun Mount M45 (With Armor)

In August 1944 in New Guinea, skipper Rex Anderson of PT156, with the help of a gunners mate named Gaddy, installed a quad 50 mount to replace the stern 20 mm gun. Rex reported the fire power of this mount was impressive, but used a tremendous amount of ammunition. *Courtesy of Stephen G. Stehling*

Close up of MK 2, 20 mm mount on PT157. *Courtesy of Wayne Traxel*

Close up of the MK 2, 20 mm mount developed in the NY Navy on PT156. *Courtesy of Wayne Traxel*

The quad 50 mount was installed at the port side foredeck of PT195 and has one crewman leaning over it. *Courtesy of Stephen G. Stehling*

Close up picture of the 40 mm gun mounted on the stern of a PT boat. *Courtesy of William Maloney*

This is an unloaded 37 mm gun on a PT boat. *Courtesy of William Maloney*

16

Engine Room

Engine Room of PT9. *Courtesy of Frank Andruss*

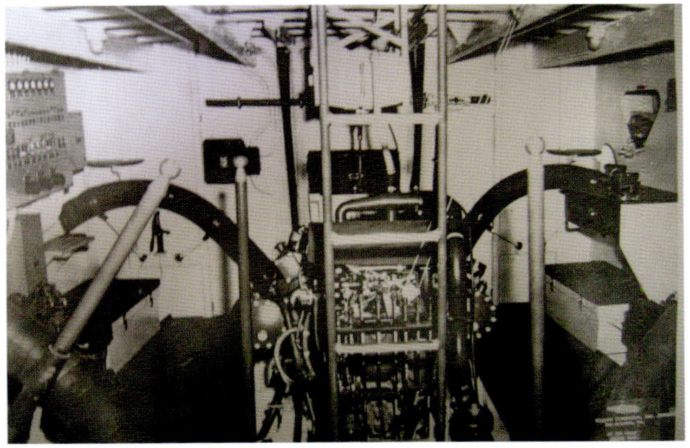

This is PT631's (Higgins PT boat) engine room. *Courtesy of Jerry Gilmartin*

Pictured is another view of PT631's engine room. *Courtesy of Jerry Gilmartin*

This is a V12 Packard marine engine carburetor. *Courtesy of Bill Maloney*

Higgins PT796 08 Packard 4M 2500 W-14 V12 supercharged marine engine. *Courtesy of Bill Maloney*

17

Exports

They were decommissioned and transferred to the USSR *Courtesy of PT Boat Museum*

PT boat on board SS *Stanvoc Captewon* bound for Australia.
Courtesy of William C. Quinby

MTB 376 was built by Annapolis Yacht Yard under lend lease agreement.
Courtesy of Imperial War Museum

MTB 422 was the former US PT 92 of the Higgins type. She was armed with a 40 mm gun aft, a 20 mm gun amidships, and two twin .50 cal. machine guns abreast the bridge. *Courtesy of Imperial War Museum*

American PT boats serving with the British fleet were credited with sinking three Axis vessels off Libya. Furthermore, they evacuated several hundred British soldiers and sailors from Tobruk under heavy shell fire and bombing. *Courtesy of Elco*

In March 1941, 77 footer Elco boats (PT 10 through PT 19) were transferred to the Royal Navy as MTBs 258 through 268. MTB 263 is seen undergoing trials by Elco. *Courtesy of the PT Boat Museum*

PT 731 Elco SO' was sent to Russia. Note the Higgins compressed air torpedo launch tube. Notice the Russian officers watching the proceedings. All except PT731 were shipped in "knock down" condition for assembly in Russia. *Courtesy of Frank Andrusso*

9 ELCOS and 1 Vosper returned by the Russians are moored in Bremherhaven, Germany, in 1956. According to records these are 731 series boats that were returned between July 2-14, 1955. The Russian Navy returned a number (23 to be exact) of lend-lease Elco PTs and some Vospers, turning them over to use at Flensburg or Lubeck, Germany, in 1956. *Courtesy of Ted Walther*

Pictured is VA Adm. Sohn Won Yil, ROK Navy, at the helm of a PT boat during a speed trial run in Sasebo Harbor, Japan. *Courtesy of Jeff Davidson.*

Personnel of the ROK Navy stand at attention on board a PT boat while the Korean national anthem is played. Four patrol torpedo boats were added to the ROK Navy when V. Adm. Won IL Sohn, ROKN, accepted the vessels from US Naval authorities in Sasebo, Japan.

PT boats making high speed runs and turns in Sasebo Harbor, Japan. The boats (PT613, 616, 619, and 620) were transferred to the ROK Navy by the US Navy. *Courtesy of Jeff Davidson*

Manned by an ROK Navy Crew, PT boat 26 (Korea) attacks the east coast of North Korea with a 5 inch rocket. *Courtesy of Jeff Davidson*

18

Models

This is a model built by John R. Haynes in 1/24 scale. John Haynes is Britain's leading professional maker of model ships. He has been building model ships commercially for the last 30 years and specializes in steel ships from 1860 to the present day. The hulls are made from fiberglass with metal-plated timber to stimulate the decks. Many of the tiny fittings, such as staircases and stanchions, are photo-etched. John's work is exhibited in London's National Maritime Museum, the Imperial War Museum, and the Science Museum in England, as well as the USS *Missouri* in Pearl Harbor. Many models are also in private collections, particularly in the United States. *Courtesy of John R. Haynes*

This PT171 model was built by Alex Johnson. The model is the Revell PT109 with White Ensign Models' photo-etched details, John R. Haynes guns, and White Ensign Models' paints. *Courtesy of T. Garth Connelly*

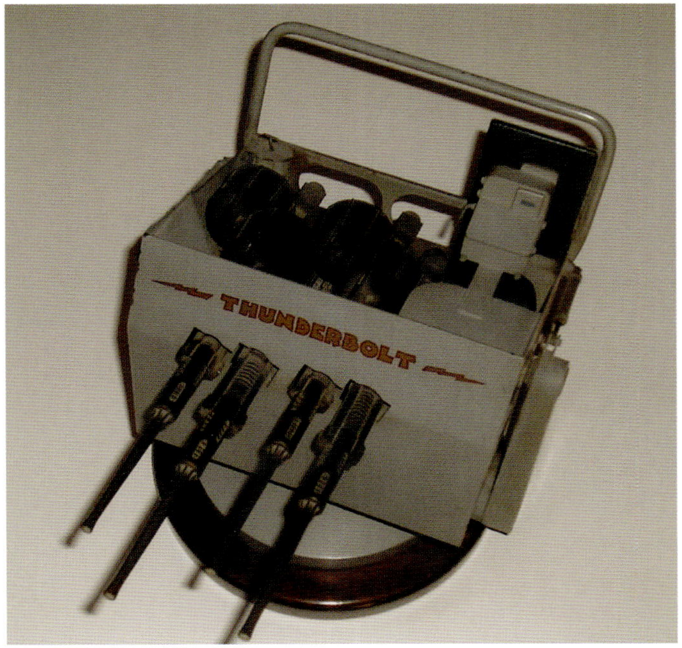

This model of a Thunderbolt is an Elco original made by their best modeler, Don Rosencrantz. All metal, it swivels on its base and elevates freely. *Courtesy of Ed B*

This is an image of an Elco boat early panel generated by Jeff D. for serious modelers. *Courtesy of Jeff D.*

This is a scratch built 1:20 scale PT41 model built by Patrick Matthews that was completed in 2006. Hull construction is dual-diagonal planking over frames (just like the original) sealed with a light weight fiberglass skin. The curvaceous cabin is built like a model airplane fuselage, using stringers over frames with balsa and plywood skin. The model of Elco's unique cradle was built from copies of Elco drawings from the National Archives. *Courtesy of Patrick Matthews*

This type of model was made to order for the Navy, Pentagon, and the White House by SDmodelworks (www.SDModelWorks.com) with incredible attention to detail and museum quality workmanship. The scale is 1/40 and the model is 21.1 inches long. The hull is hand carved from kiln-dried mahogany. Other parts are made from a variety of woods, putty, resin, and metals. Every model includes brass pedestals, a polished mahogany base board, and a brass name plate. *Courtesy of Captain Brad Poulos*

This model of PT 109 is in 1⁄4" = 1' – 0" scale and built by Stephen W. Henninger of American Marine Model Gallery. The model's hull is constructed of basswood with solid deck house components and masts and fittings of Britannia, brass, polycarbonate, and aluminum. The model is mounted on brass pedestals with a mahogany baseboard with inlaid satinwood and glazed cover trimmed in brass. American Marine Model Gallery specializes in sales of exceptional one of a kind ship models for worldwide corporate collections. *Courtesy of American Marine Model Gallery (www.shipmodel.com)*

This is a model of PT 18 built by Mike Salzano in 1/72 scale. The hull is from the Airfix RAF 63 ft. rescue boat kit. The hull was lengthened and widened. The deck is made of basswood, and everything above the deck was scratch built or vacuum formed. *Courtesy of Mike Salzano*

PT777, an 80 foot Elco 1/4 inch scale, was built for the US Navy by Elco. It was donated to the museum by Charles D. Case. This boat was never built due to the end of the conflict and the contract was cancelled. The detail in this model is excellent and it is made of soft metal. *Courtesy of Donald R. Shannon*

This is a PT11 in 1:48 scale with a wood strip hull donated by Martin E. Hill. It is located at Battleship Cove, Fall River, MA. *Courtesy of Donald R. Shannon*

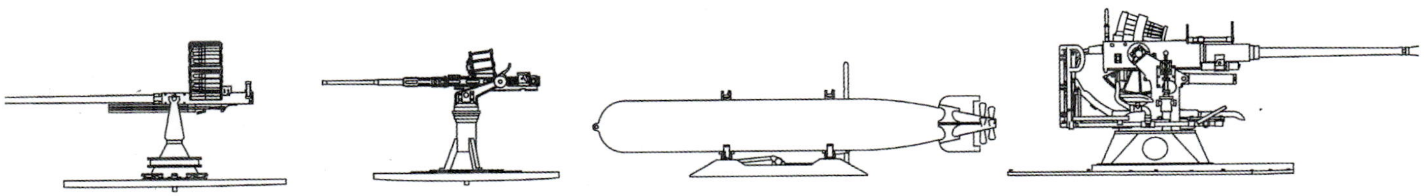

This is the finished Italeri plastic kit model of the late Elco PT596 in 1:35 scale with aluminum gun barrels for the 20 mm and 40 mm gun and various sheet metal fittings. This model has a large single hull thick-wall molding. The instruction booklet displays clear 3 dimensional and precise drawings, which is an art in and of itself. *Courtesy of Italeri*

PT 495 of Ron 33 was assigned to patrol Ailape-Wewak in New Guinea about July 1944. On their second patrol they spotted four enemy barges in column formation. With PT 495 firing on the Japanese barges and shore batteries, Jim J. Shaw, Jr., MoMM2c, was fatally hit and killed. Jim was known by the rest of the crew as a perfect PT man. PT 495 was named "Gentleman Jim" in his honor. *Courtesy of Raymond Strand and Ed Ducati*

This cased model of PT596 was built by Jerry Gilmartin from the 1/35 scale Italieri plastic kit. Several parts were made by Eduord Inc. of the Czech Republic, including .50 caliber ammo belts and .40 mm ammo clips to the railing of the .40 mm Bofors gun mount. *Courtesy of Jerry Gilmartin*

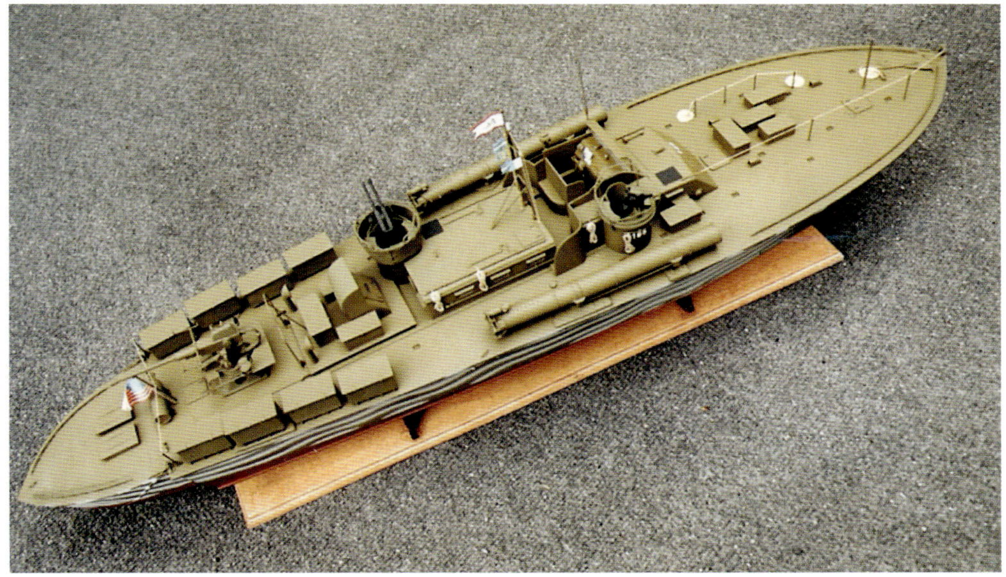

This is PT196 scratch built by Stan Pienkowski. The boat was built using photographs only. The scale is 1/32, and every fitting was scratch built. The hull and superstructures were made from wood using an Elco blueprint. *Courtesy of Frank Andruss*

Right and following: This realistic diorama of PT596 was constructed from a 1/35 scale Italeri Elco 80' and diorama accessories and photo-etched metal parts from Royal Model di Roberto Reale (www.royalmodel.com) of Italy. Every part is made to provide maximum detail and fidelity. The after market parts are the frame of the 37 mm gun feeder, parts of the .50 caliber machine gun, and parts of the torpedo launcher. Etched barrels for the .50 caliber machine gun can be made from furnished parts (for additional information, see *Military Miniature in Review* (MMIR), no. 50 and 51). *Courtesy of Robert Reale from Royal Model and Military Miniature in Review*

596

This is basically a Revel kit 1/72 scale with the following modifications: 1. White Ensign Model (WEM) photo-etch set was used. Some of these are still brass colored in the photo. 2. Reworked the cockpit area with styrene. There were lots of small details added using brass tubing and styrene. 3. The depression rails were soldered from annealed brass and formed. 4. The .50 cal machine guns were replaced with Aries resin guns because they had the flash suppression molded in. 5. Scratch built depth charges from brass tubing and mounted inside the WEM photo-etch rack. 6. Add the Hohn Haynes . 20 mm stand and gun. 7. The 37 mm gun on the bow is from WEM. *Courtesy of David Waples*

This is a Revell Model of PT109 near completion. *Courtesy of David Waples*

PT41 was presented to Lt. John D. Bulkeley by Henry Sutphen of Elco while Bulkeley was visiting the Elco plant in Bayonne, NJ. *Courtesy of Frank Andruss*

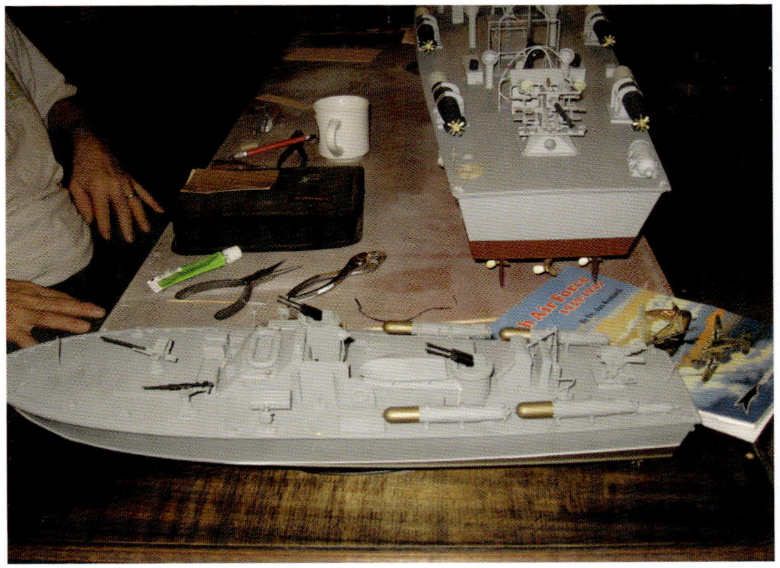

Elco Factory Model made by the famous Don Rosencrantz. It is made entirely from machined metal pieces. The man in the photo is Stan Pienkowski, who builds most of the Exhibit boats. *Courtesy of Frank Andruss*

One of the featured attractions at the Elco-Packard Exhibit being held at the Bankers Trust Company in New York is a model of PT41. This boat was commanded by Lt. John D. Bulkeley, who took General Douglas MacArthur from the Philippines in a daring rescue mission. Looking on are four members of a PT Squadron now on leave. From right to left: Lt. Clark Faulkner, USNR of Kansas City; Lt. W. R. Barrett, New York City; Lt. J. J. Cross, Laurel, MS; and Lt. William Elson of Providence, RI.

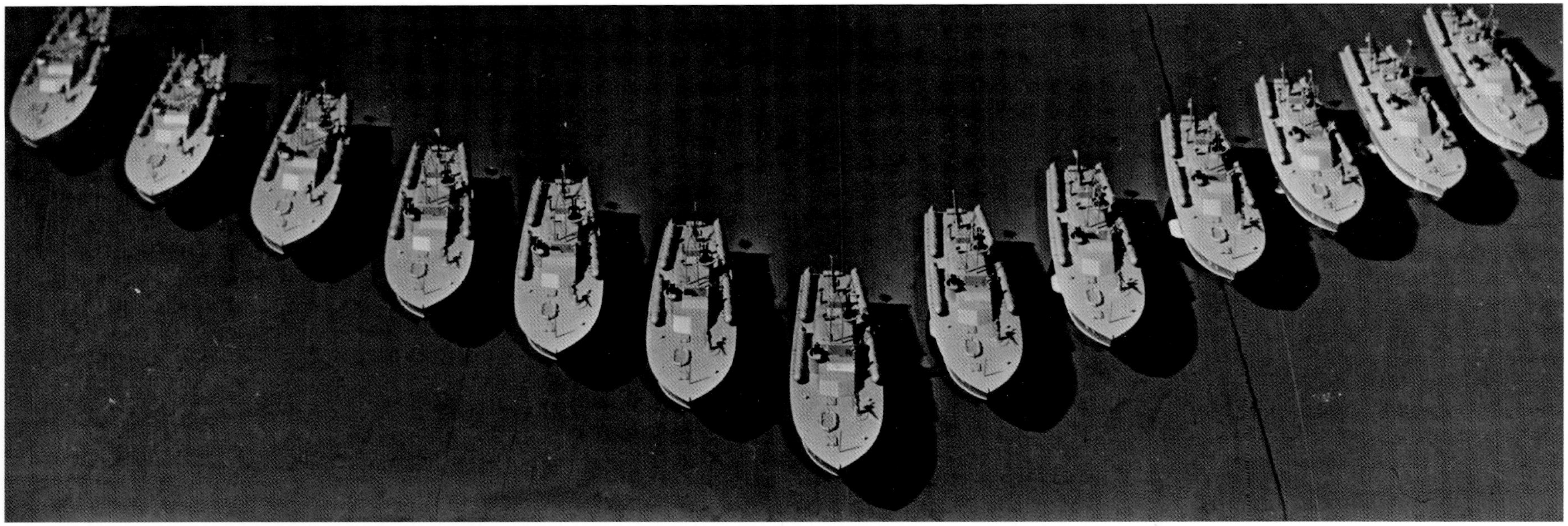

Models PT 117, Elco fleet of model PTs in V formation.
Courtesy of Elco

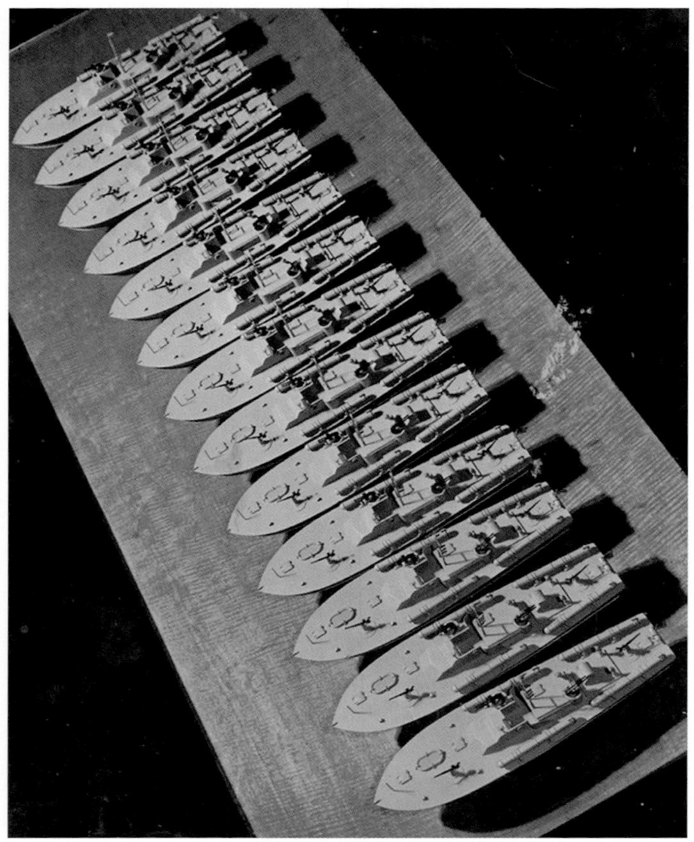

Mass production of Elco 80' models at the Elco factory.
Courtesy of Frank Andruss

This model, presented to Lt. John D. Bulkeley, was built by Don Rosencrantz, the top model builder at Elco. It is still in existence as part of the Bulkeley estate. *Courtesy of Frank J. Andruss, Sr.*

This is another view of the PT41 model showing the detail of the model. This model was made from mostly metal with all machined parts. *Courtesy of Frank J. Andruss* Sr.

Pictured is a drawing of the turret and twin .50 machine gun mount on a PT boat using CAD (Computer Aided Design) to create a virtual model in three dimensions that can be viewed from any angle. It is based on the actual dimensions of the original factory drawings. The depth of research to build a museum quality model is limitless. *Courtesy of Jeff Davidson.*

This model was built by Lawrence Cohen DDS of Wappingers Falls, NY, 12590. The entire model, except the hull, was built with plastic and brass rods. He spent a year on construction. This model is in 1/32 scale. *Courtesy of Lawrence Cohen*

A standard 1/72 scale Revell kit with the zebra type pattern camouflage properly applied by Alfonso M. Berlana of Alicante, Spain, looks like a museum piece even under close scrutiny. *Courtesy of Alfonso M. Berlana*

This builder's model of PT 41, in 1/16 scale, is on loan to the MacArthur Memorial at Norfolk, Virginia. *Courtesy of the US Naval Academy Museum via James W. Zobel and Don Preul*

This model is constructed according to the specifications and directions as outlined by Comet Metal Products, under the brand name "Authenticast." This company was one of several model companies which supplied naval and aircraft models to the Defense Department during WWII. There were five such models commissioned by the Elco Naval Division of Electric Boat Co. of Bayonne, NJ, in 1945. The 1/48 model's full hull is constructed from a metal form with wood and/or metal trim details. It includes a good variety of machined or cast metal parts and assemblies per this vessel's design, and is fitted out with all appropriate armament, i.e. four 21 inch MK-13 Torpedoes, one 40mm MK3, one 37mm, one 20mm, two twin 50 cal., two five inch rocket launchers, snips boat, deck gear, vents, smoke canister, ammo lockers, antennas, search light, mast, and other details specified in the ship's design. *Courtesy of John F. Molnar*

(#82 and #83) VICTOR, multiple copies of #83 and none are a picture of a model Models of Elco and Higgins boats built by Tim Howard (1/32 scale) in the 1980s, before Italeri's 1/35 scale PT596 hit the drawing board. Tim started Howard Enterprise and sold kits to modelers. *Courtesy of Victor Chun*

Operational "model" from the motion picture "PT 109." This rebuilt PT109 was one of three converted from USAF 85 foot Air Sea Rescue boats by Miami Shipbuilding. The Navy department supplied the weapons. *Courtesy of Warner Bros*

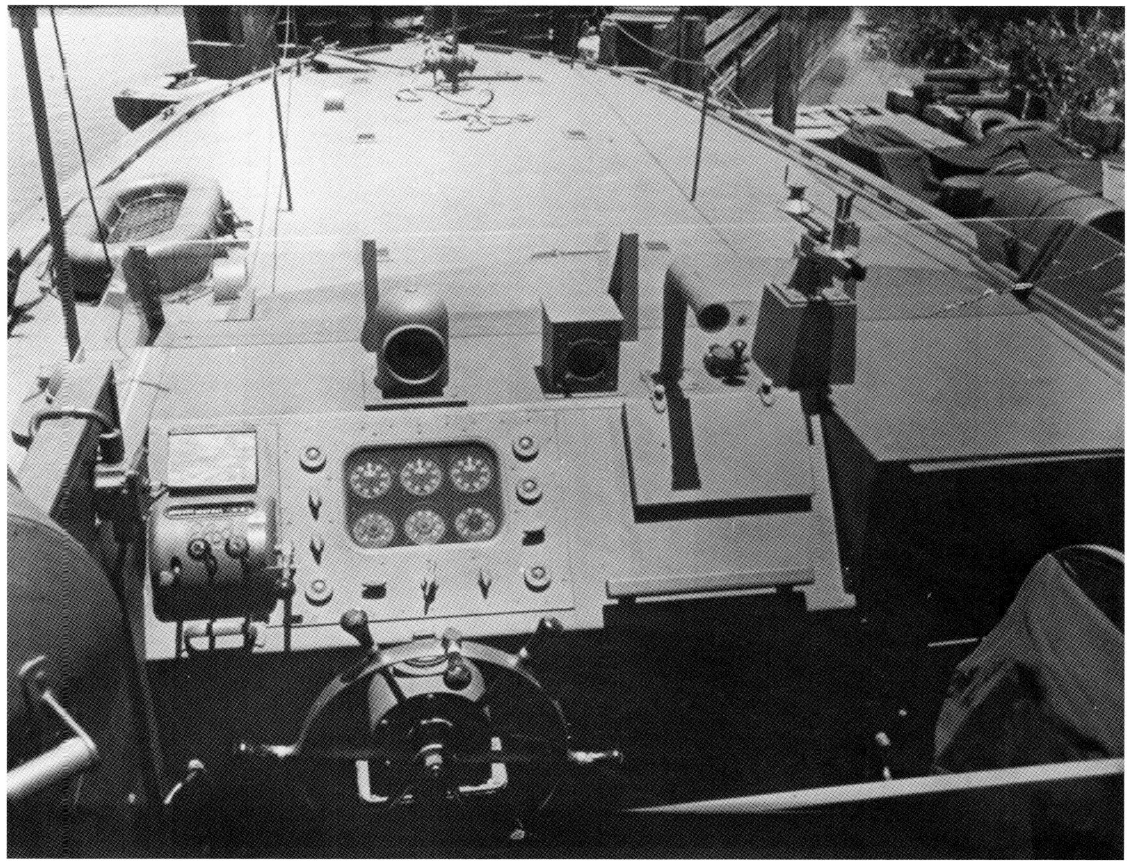

Pictured is a model of a life size cockpit for the motion picture "PT 109" built by Miami Shipbuilding. Note the seldom seen torpedo director just behind the windshield. *Courtesy of Warner Bros*

This is Miami Shipbuilding's model for the motion picture "PT 109."

This is a deck view of Miami Shipbuilding's model for the motion picture "PT 109."

This 1/32 scale museum quality PT157 model with extreme detail was built by Bridgeman Carney from scratch. This model showcases the many details of PT157 as it was in the summer of 1943. A variety of resources were used to ensure the accuracy of the details, including discussions with members of the original PT157 crew, a PC CAD program to check dimensions and insure parts would assemble properly, and numerous PT dedicated websites. This model does run on water, with radio control, and has rotating .50 cal and 20 mm rear deck guns to simulate the boat in "mission mode". During the six years of construction, the builder took over 2500 pictures to document the step by step construction for his own later reference; however, later he began to write notebooks about building this PT157 model. These notebooks now contain over 350 chosen photos in over 250 pages in four volumes. *Courtesy of Bridgeman Carney*

USS *Oyster Bay*, AGP-6, Motor Torpedo Boat Tender depicted as tending to PT boats of Motor Torpedo Boat Squadron (MTB) Ron 33 at Leyte Gulf, Philippines, in November 1944. The USS *Oyster Bay* model was converted and modified from the 1/350 Scale Resin Model kit of the USS *Mackinac* AVP-13, Seaplane Tender Small, manufactured by Iron Shipwrights, Inc. and incorporating scratch building of many features of the model, as well as the use of many after market ship model accessories. The PT boats were modified from 1/350 Scale Resin Model kits of the 80' Elco PT109 manufactured by White Ensign Models. Built by Carl T. Musselman of Omaha, Nebraska, 2010. *Courtesy of Carl T. Musselman*

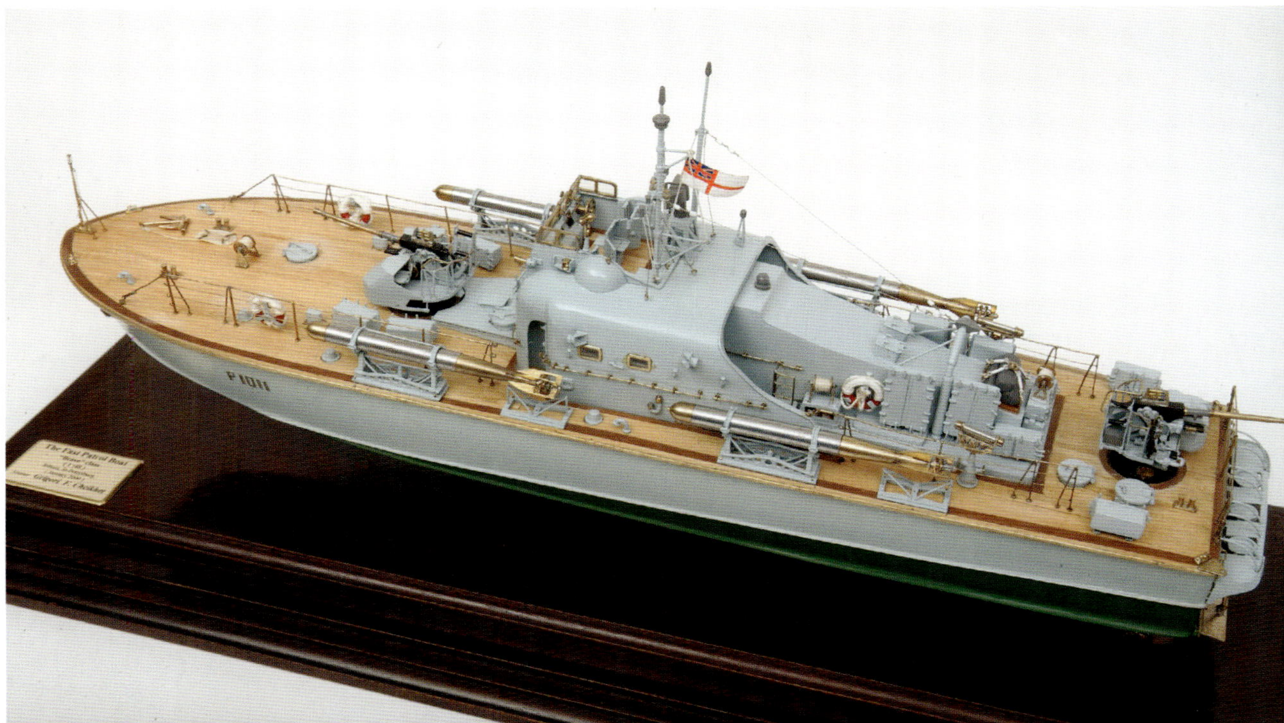

Although this book is about American PT boats, this model of HMS *Borderer* (P10110) built by Grigorif Cheikhet (28 1/2" x 14" x 10" size) was spotted at an auction. It is so realistic that I felt duty bound to include it here. *Courtesy of Bonhams & Butterfields via Staci Smith and Julie Saunders*

"These twin .50s provide PT enthusiasts with a level of detail not offered in cast metal or resin. With a variable-position carriage, upper ammo guides, lower ammo guides, dual trigger mechanism and ammo belts, this kit has the works. Nimble fingers, patience and four to five hours building time are a must."

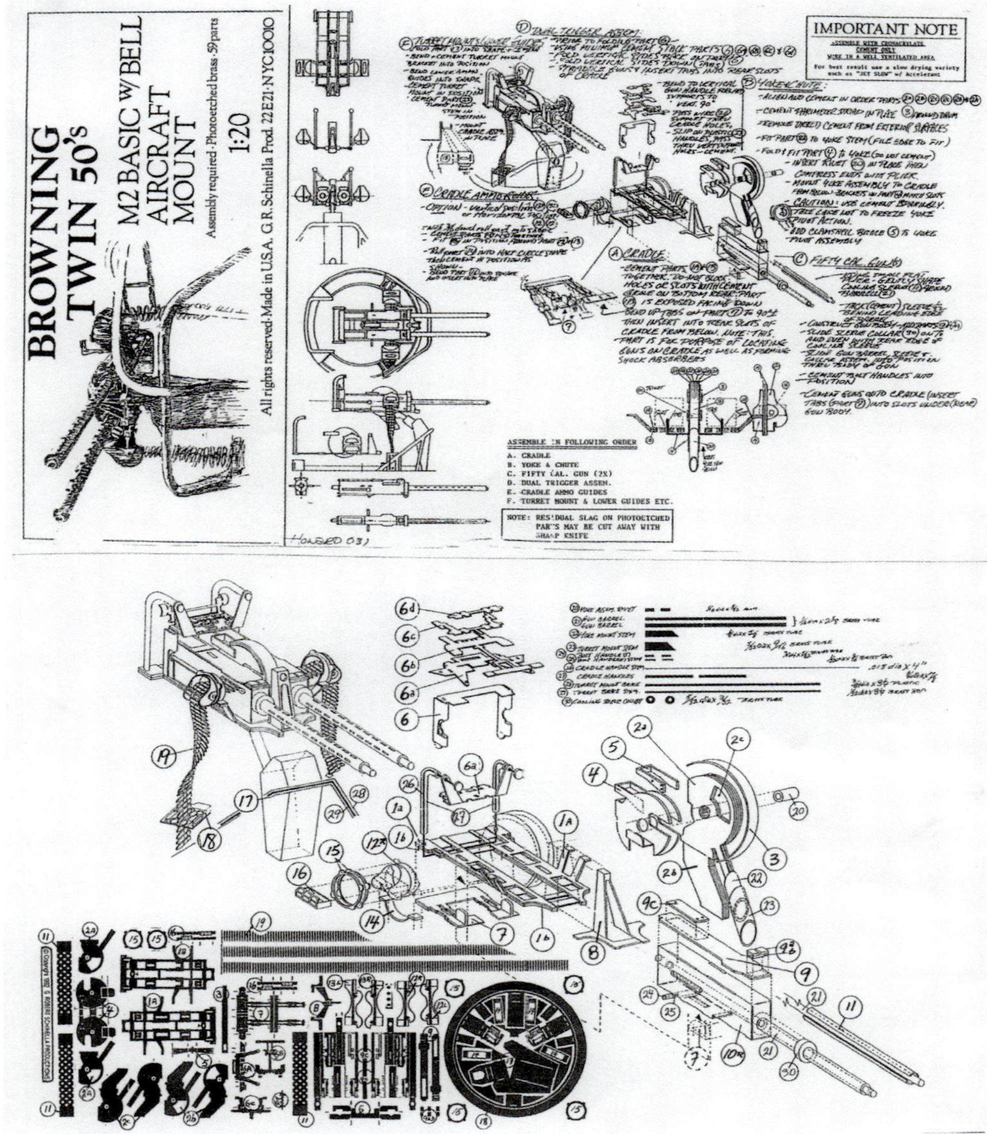

Back in 1993, this kit of the twin .50 cal. machine gun turret in 1/20 and 1/30 scales was selling for only $29.95, including postage. All recent efforts to contact Mr. Schinella failed. These drawings, included in the kit, show the intricate instructions to assemble the twin 50s. *Courtesy of Jerry Beasley*

This photo shows the detail of the PT157 port side turret with its twin .50 caliber guns. This required hundreds of individual pieces (not including the ammunition and ammo belts) to complete. This gun set, ammo boxes, ammo racks, and seat back rotate to demonstrate the actual action of the turret gunner. *Courtesy of Bridgeman Carney*

19

Hudson River Tour

With the end of WWII in the fall of 1945, seven PT boats of Ron 42 (PT486, 487, 545, 557, 558, 559, and 615) left Melville, RI, and went up the Hudson River heading for Chicago on a War Bond Drive. They stopped by West Point on October 20, 1945, for the football game between the PT Night Raiders and the West Point team (Army 55, PT 13). Previously, on 15 September, the PT Night Raiders defeated Worcester Polytechnic Institute (the author's alma mater) 32-0.

Ron 42 PT boats going up the Hudson River during the fall of 1945 for a bond drive in Chicago. This picture was taken from the shoreline in the Riverdale section of Bronx, NY, where this author used to live. Please note the George Washington Bridge in the background. *Courtesy of Frank Andruss*

PT557 on the Hudson River, heading up to Detroit after the war had ended. Milt Donadt is manning the 37mm canon on the bow. Mr. Donadt was stationed near Boston, and volunteered to take the PT boats to Detroit for display. The boats were brought back through the locks and ended up at the Brooklyn Navy yard. *Courtesy of Milt Donadt*

Melville, RI, was the starting point of the journey to Detroit, MI. *Courtesy of Milt Donadt*

This is a PT boat going full speed ahead toward Detroit. *Courtesy of Milt Donadt*

Notice the radar mast tilted back to allow clearance under the bridges. *Courtesy of William Maloney*

The large round "thing" is the radar dome lowered for clearance under the bridges. *Courtesy of William Maloney*

PT557 was one of the four boats equipped with the Thunderbolt. This was taken at Little Fall, NY. *Courtesy of Milt Donadt via Wfyimmerman*

Navy Day, Fall 1945, in the Erie Canal lock en route to Cleveland. *Photo by George Frick*

Pictured is the lock at Little Fall, NY. *Courtesy of Milt Donadt via Wfyimmerman*

This is PT486, -487, and -545 in the Welland Canal between Lake Erie and Ontario. *Courtesy of Frank Andruss*

PT557, -487, and -545 (from left to right front row) moored along outside lock #17 on the way to Detroit, October 1945. *Courtesy of Frank Andruss*

PT boats in the locks. *Courtesy of Al Ross*

Navy Day, October 27, 1945, in Detroit, Michigan. *Courtesy of the PT Boat Museum*

PT 603, Ron 41, open for public inspection, with PTs 604 and 606 at Michigan Avenue Bridge in Chicago for Navy Day. *Courtesy of the PT Boat Museum*

20

Drawings

Due to a fire at the Elco plant in Bayonne, NJ (see Chapter 23), all of the original drawings of the Elco PT boat were destroyed. Fortunately, prints are still available in museums and from individuals. Included in this chapter are never before published isometric drawings of the interior and exterior of a PT boat by the great graphic designer and illustrator, Dick Washichek. Mr. Washichek stated that he was able to create these amazing drawings by "drawing and plotting by hand using proportional dividers, parallel edge and triangles. Once the pencil drawing is completed, I then scan the image onto my computer and open the scanned image into Adobe Illustrator®. I then hand trace the scanned isometric with the pen tool and save it as an .eps file." This takes a great deal of time, and Mr. Washichek's drawings are very accurate.

PT-59

ELCO 77' - Series PT 45 - PT 68

Manufactured By Electric Boat Company, Bayonne, New Jersey - September 1941 Through January 1942

Illustrated as Shown in a Combat Photographs & Drawings

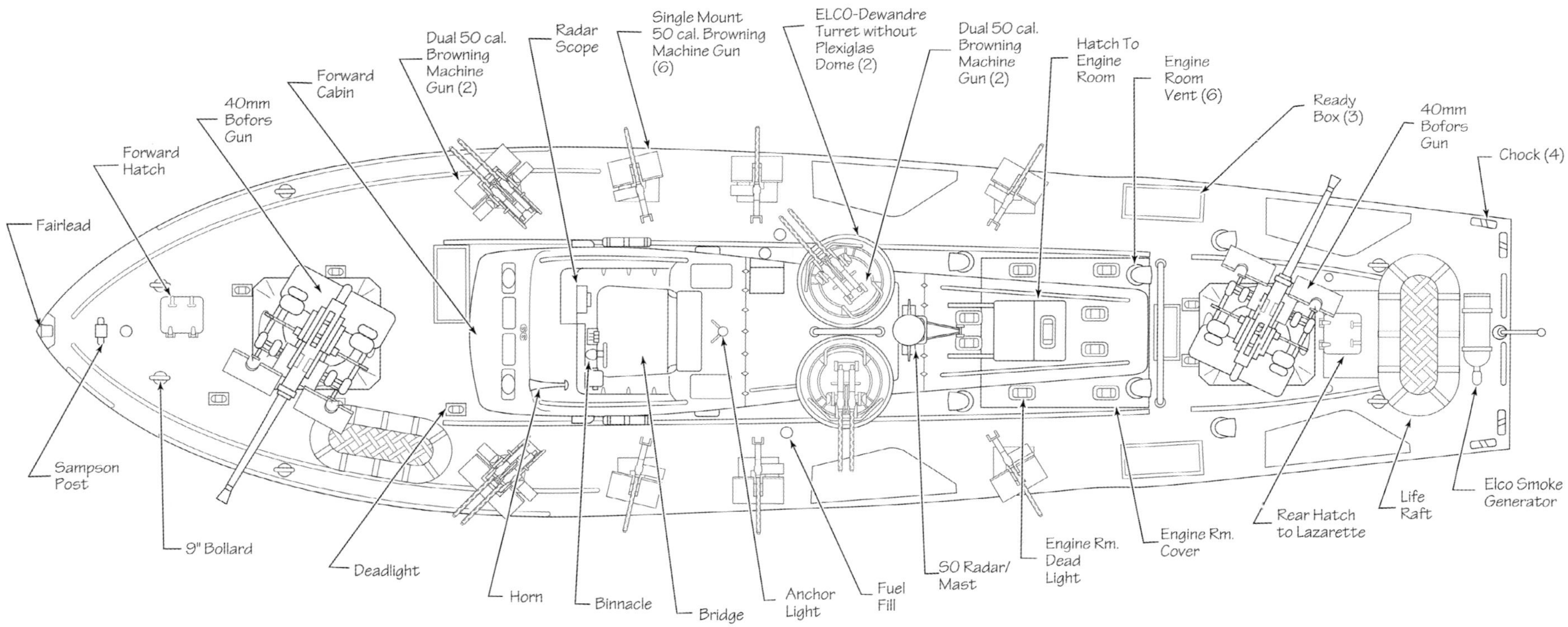

SPECIFICATIONS:

Length	77'-0"
Beam	19'-11"
Draft	4'-6"
Displacement (loaded)	46 tons
Total Fuel Capacity	3,000 gal.
Engines	(3) 1,200 HP
Top Speed	42 Knots
Propellers	3
Rudders	3

PT Boat Nickname: Gun Boat

NOTE:
Placed into Service: March 5, 1942 - at the MTB Squadrons Training Center, Ron 4.
Transferred to the Pacific with MTB Squadron: Ron 2 on May 2, 1942, then transferred to Ron 3 (2) November 11, 1943.

Illustrated & Copyrighted © 2007, by Richard J. Washichek

Courtesy of Richard J. Washichek

PT-59

ELCO 77' - Series PT 45 - PT 68

Manufactured By Electric Boat Company, Bayonne, New Jersey - September 1941 Through January 1942

Illustrated as Shown in a Combat Photographs & Drawings

SPECIFICATIONS:

Length	77'-0"
Beam	19'-11"
Draft	4'-6"
Displacement (loaded)	46 tons
Total Fuel Capacity	3,000 gal.
Engines	(3) 1,200 HP
Top Speed	42 Knots
Propellers	3
Rudders	3

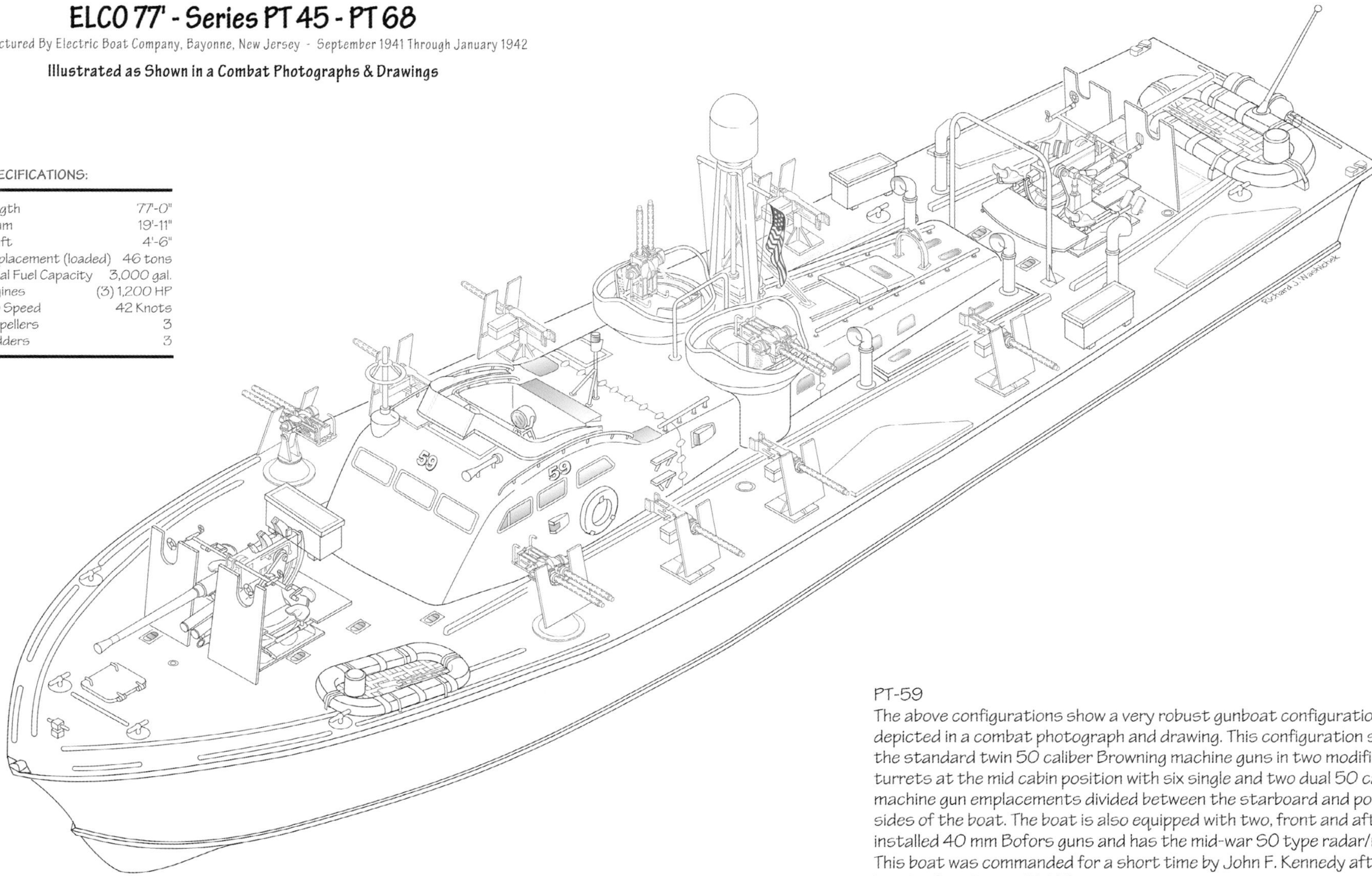

PT-59
The above configurations show a very robust gunboat configuration as depicted in a combat photograph and drawing. This configuration shows the standard twin 50 caliber Browning machine guns in two modified turrets at the mid cabin position with six single and two dual 50 caliber machine gun emplacements divided between the starboard and port sides of the boat. The boat is also equipped with two, front and aft installed 40 mm Bofors guns and has the mid-war SO type radar/mast. This boat was commanded for a short time by John F. Kennedy after he lost his first boat, PT-109.

NOTE:
Placed into Service: March 5, 1942 - at the MTB Squadrons Training Center, Ron 4.
Transferred to the Pacific with MTB Squadron: Ron 2 on May 2, 1942, then transferred to Ron 3 (2) November 11, 1943.

PT Boat Nickname: *Gun Boat*

Illustrated & Copyrighted © 2007, by Richard J. Washichek

Courtesy of Richard J. Washichek

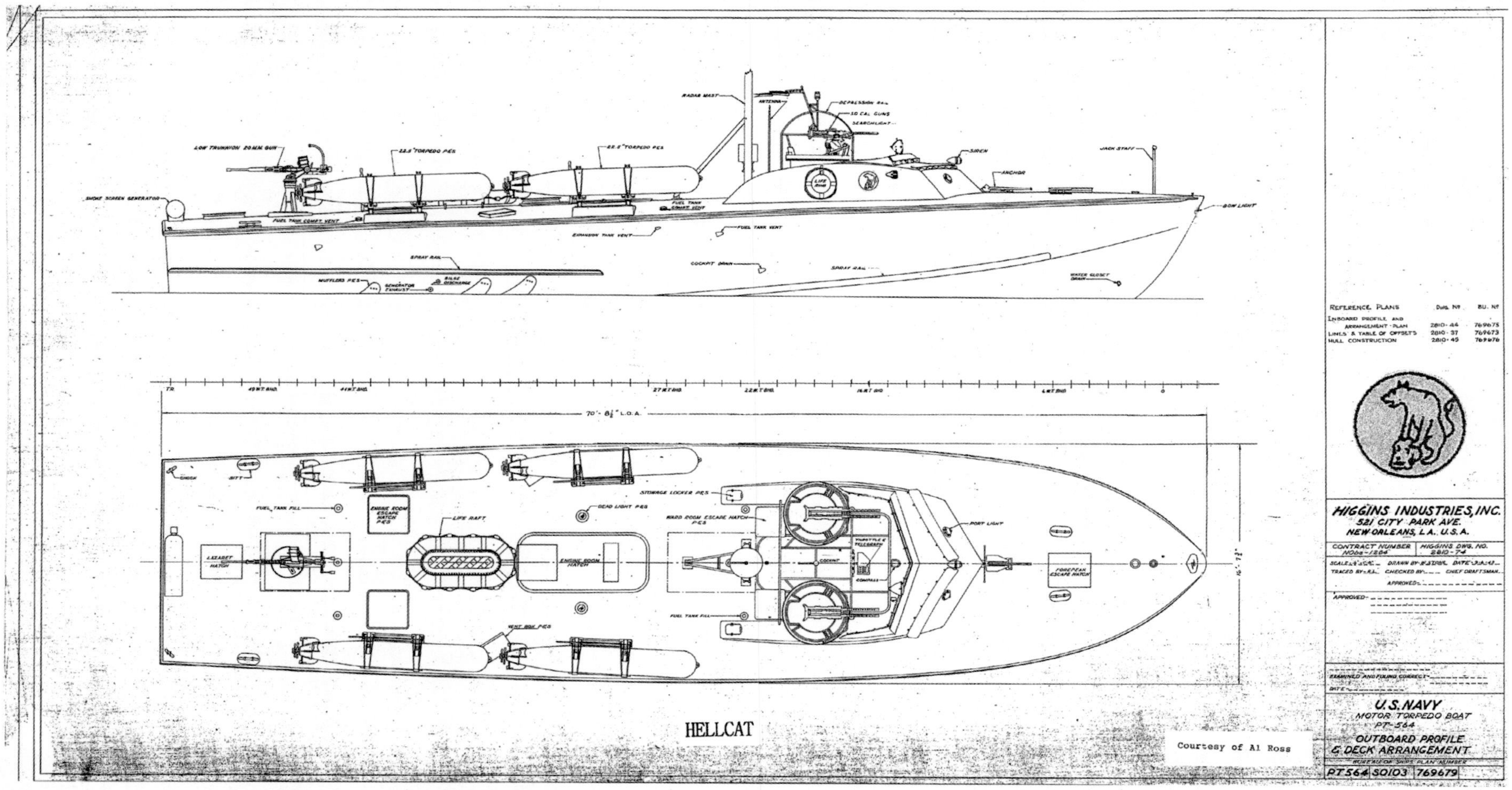

Courtesy of Al Ross

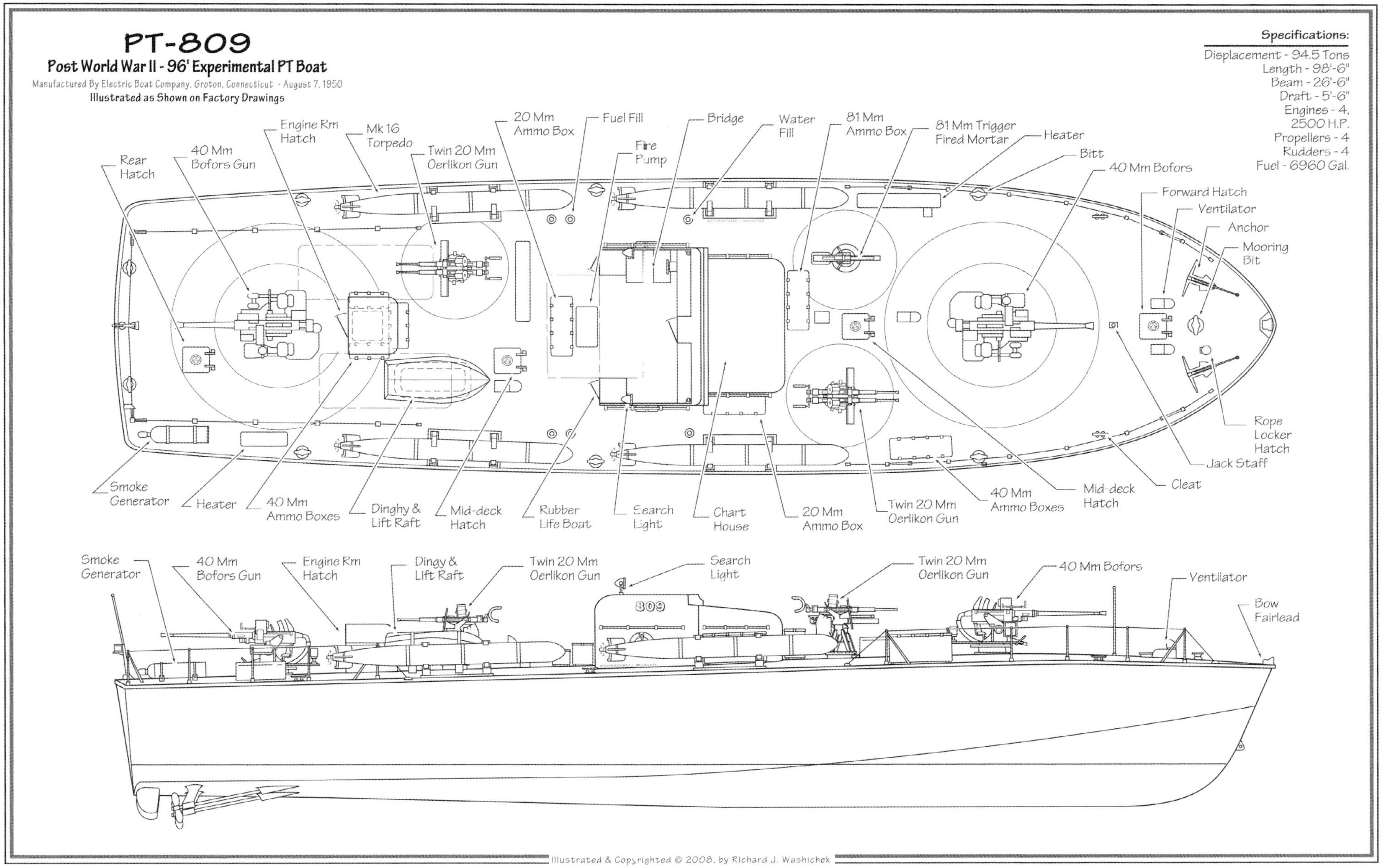

The original drawings of PT809 were lost due to the Elco fire. No more drawings can be found from the Navy Department due to their bad filing system. Recently I received a badly printed blueprint that Al Ross located 30 years ago at the Navy Historical center. This was carefully copied by graphic artist, Dick Washichek. In 1960, PT809 was used as a Presidential Yacht Escort named Guardian. It was used by the Secret Service as a chase boat for the *Noney Fitz*, the Hyannisport yacht of President Kennedy. In 1974 PT809 served as a drone retriever, DR-1. In July 1992, the Navy offered her for sale and declared her abandoned. *Courtesy of Dick Washichek and Al Ross*

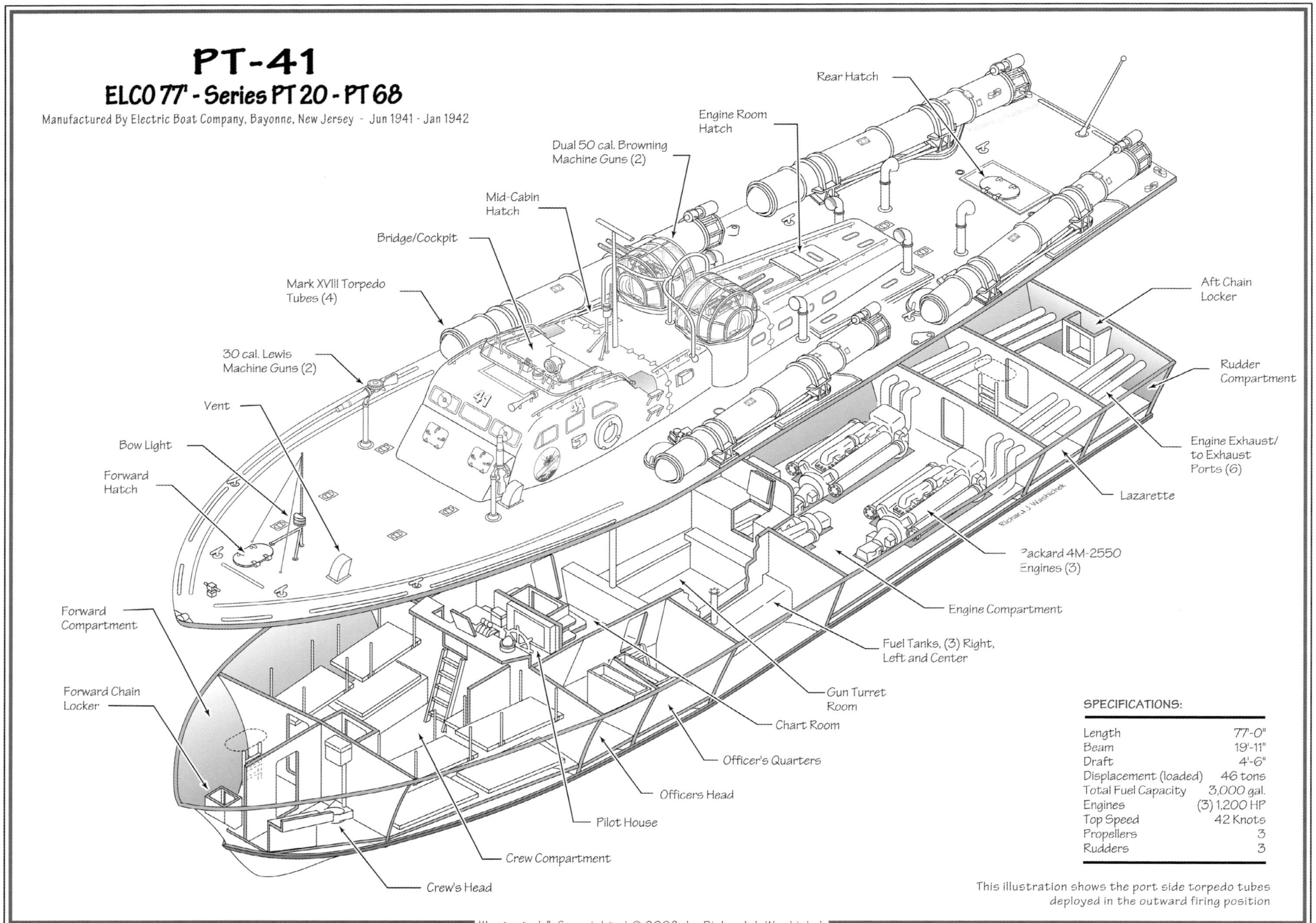

Courtesy of Richard J. Washichek

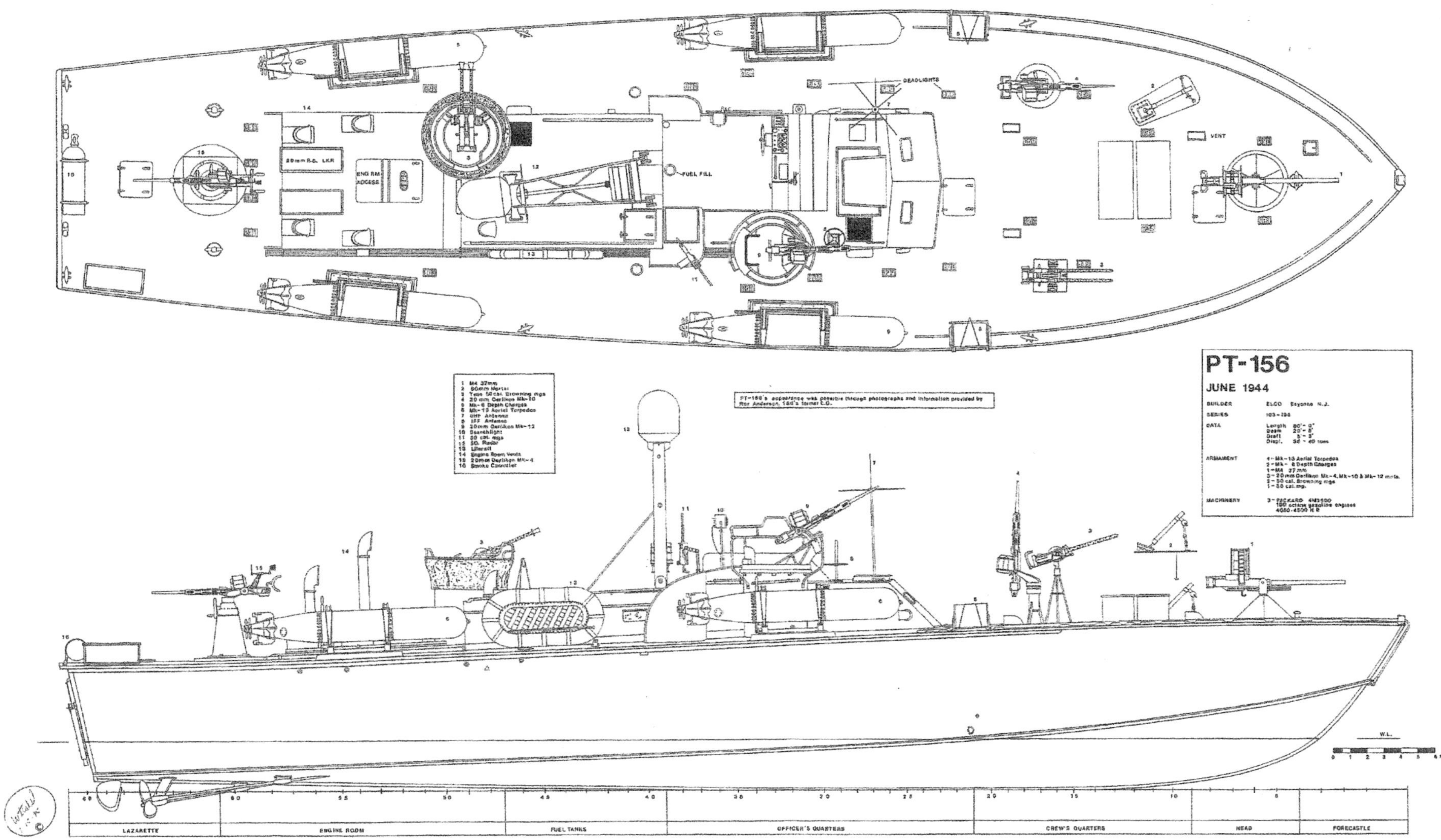

The drawing of PT156 shows this craft's appearance in June 1944 with a retrofitted MK-12, 20mm scarf ring mount in the starboard forward turret. *Courtesy of Wayne Traxel*

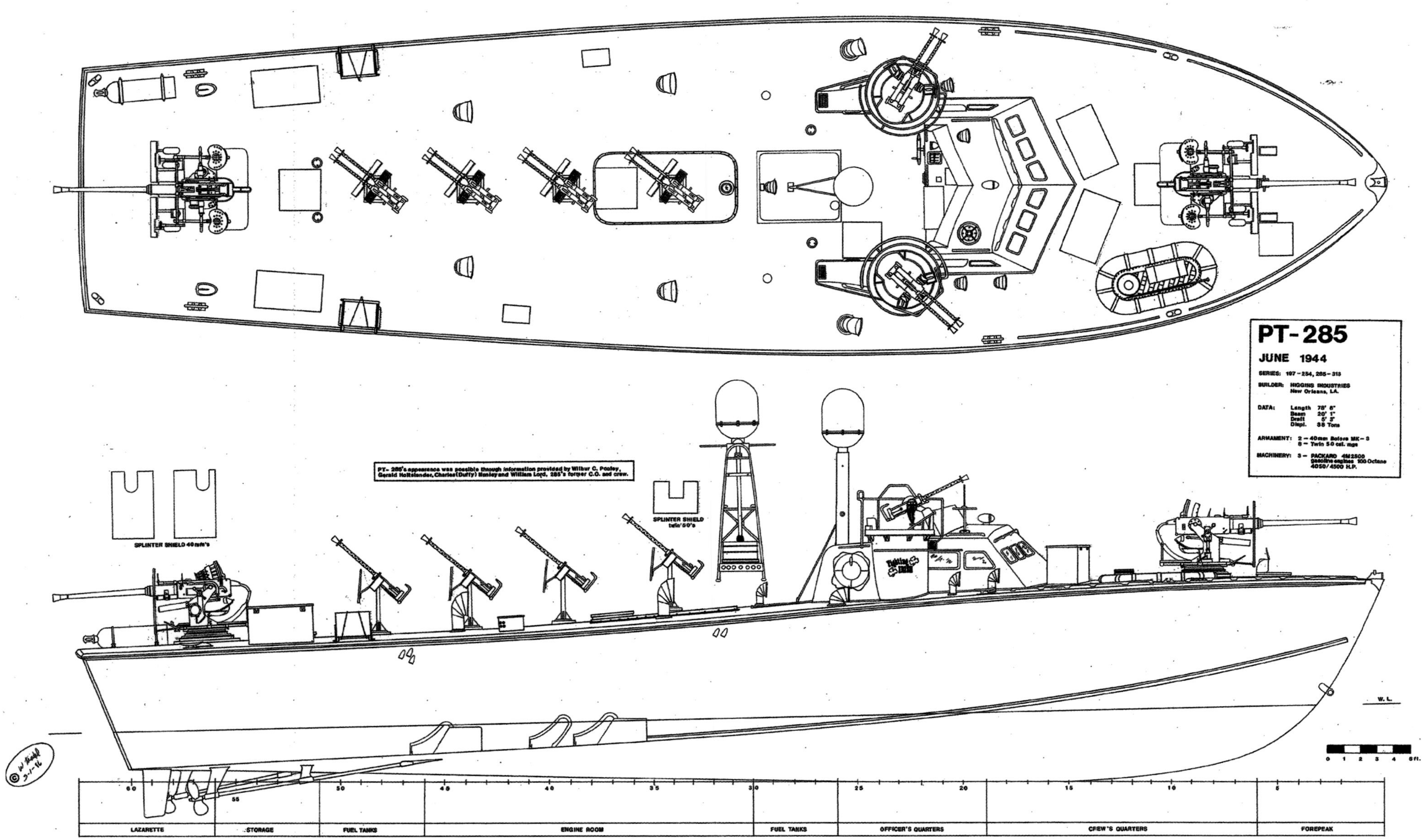

PT285 was re-fitted with heavier armament: 40mm Bofors fore and aft, and additional twin .50 cal. machine guns, seen here by the tender USS *Argonne*. The purpose for the additional firepower was to control the Japanese barges and similar shallow-draft vessels used for transporting military personnel and supplies. These vessels operated very close to shore in western Bougainville, particularly in Empress August Bay. *Courtesy of Wayne Traxel*

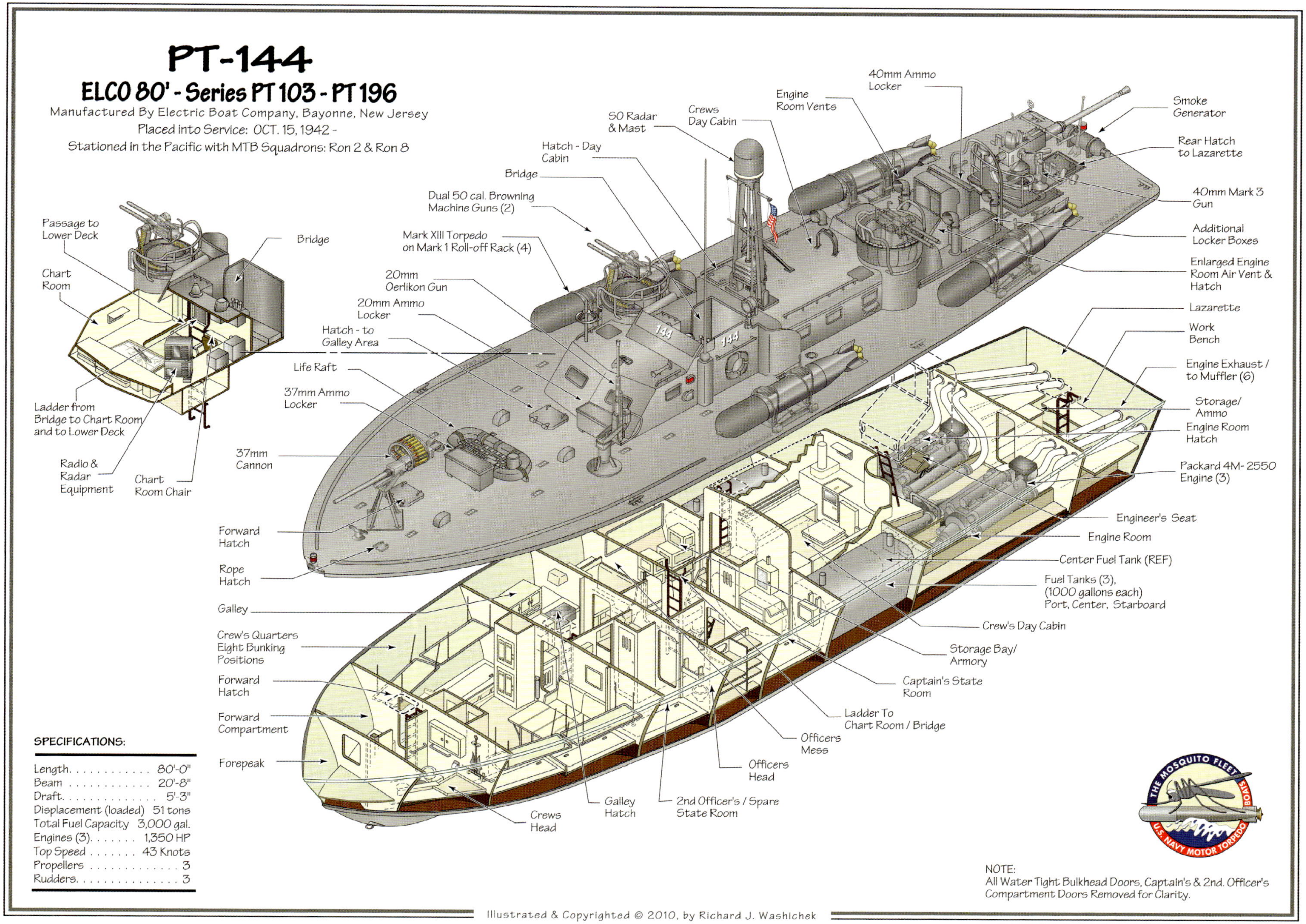

Courtesy of Richard J. Washichek

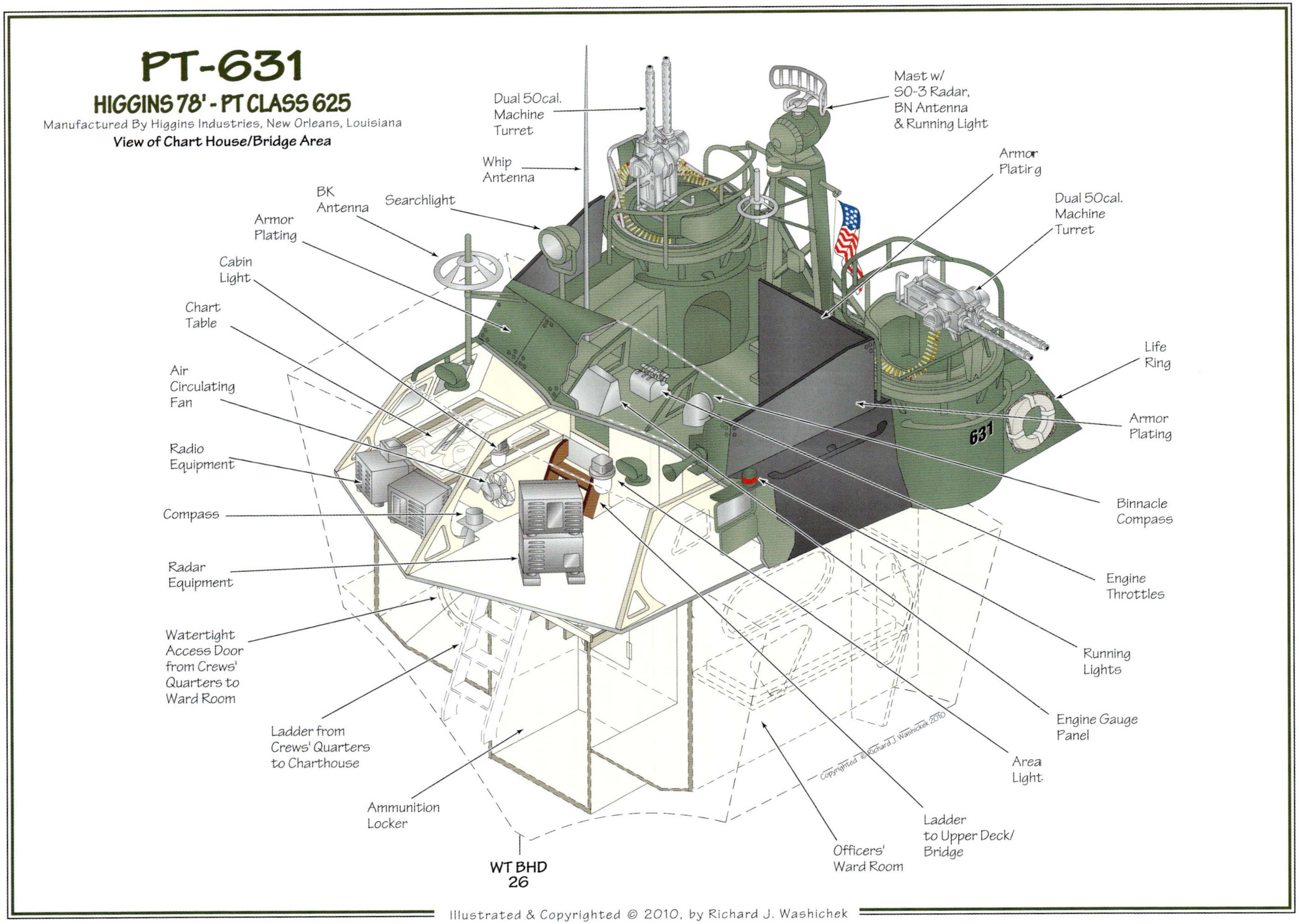

To protect the crew on the bridge, the Elco factory provided armor plating around the cockpit of their 80' boats. Some skippers had them removed to save weight, and it allowed easier access to the helm. The Higgins 78' had no armor plate, except their PT625 to PT660. Each bridge was surrounded with armor plates. Armor was attached to the wind screen, then stretched along the side and ended at the gun turret; then it did a 90 degree turn halfway across the deck. *Courtesy of Richard J. Washichek*

PT-130

ELCO 80' - Series PT 103 - PT 196

Manufactured By Electric Boat Company, Bayonne, New Jersey - 1942 Through 1943

Deck Plan - Illustrated as Shown in a Combat Photograph

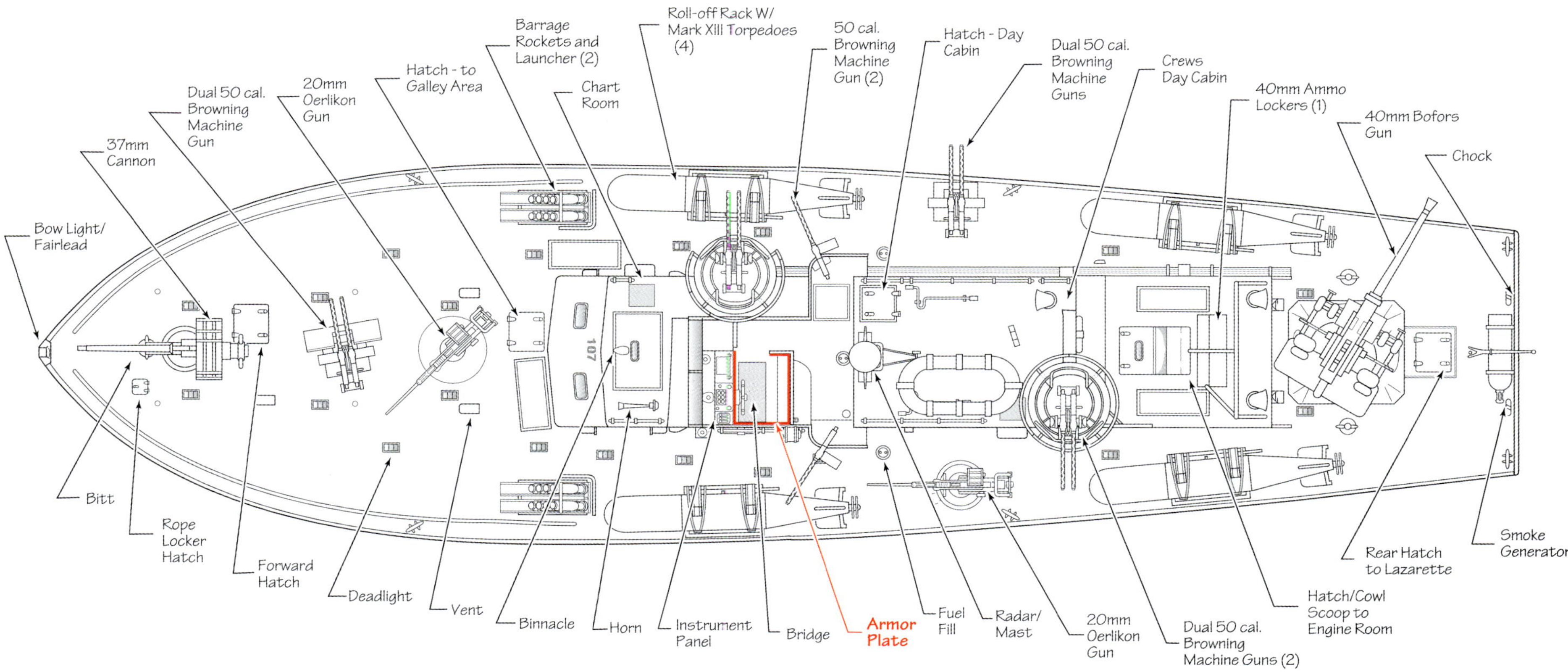

SPECIFICATIONS:

Length	80'-0"
Beam	20'-8"
Draft	5'-3"
Displacement (loaded)	51 tons
Total Fuel Capacity	3,000 gal.
Engines	(3) 1,350 HP
Top Speed	43 Knots
Propellers	3
Rudders	3

PT Boat Nickname: Raven

NOTE:

Placed into Service: Sept. 7, 1942 -

Stationed in the Pacific with MTB Squadrons: Ron 7. Transferred to Ron 8 on Feb. 15, 1945

Illustrated & Copyrighted © 2007, by Richard J. Washichek

Courtesy of Richard J. Washichek

PT-130

ELCO 80' - Series PT 103 - PT 196

Manufactured By Electric Boat Company, Bayonne, New Jersey - 1942 Through 1943

Illustrated as Shown in a Combat Photograph

SPECIFICATIONS:

Length	80'-0"
Beam	20'-8"
Draft	5'-3"
Displacement (loaded)	51 tons
Total Fuel Capacity	3,000 gal.
Engines	(3) 1,350 HP
Top Speed	43 Knots
Propellers	3
Rudders	3

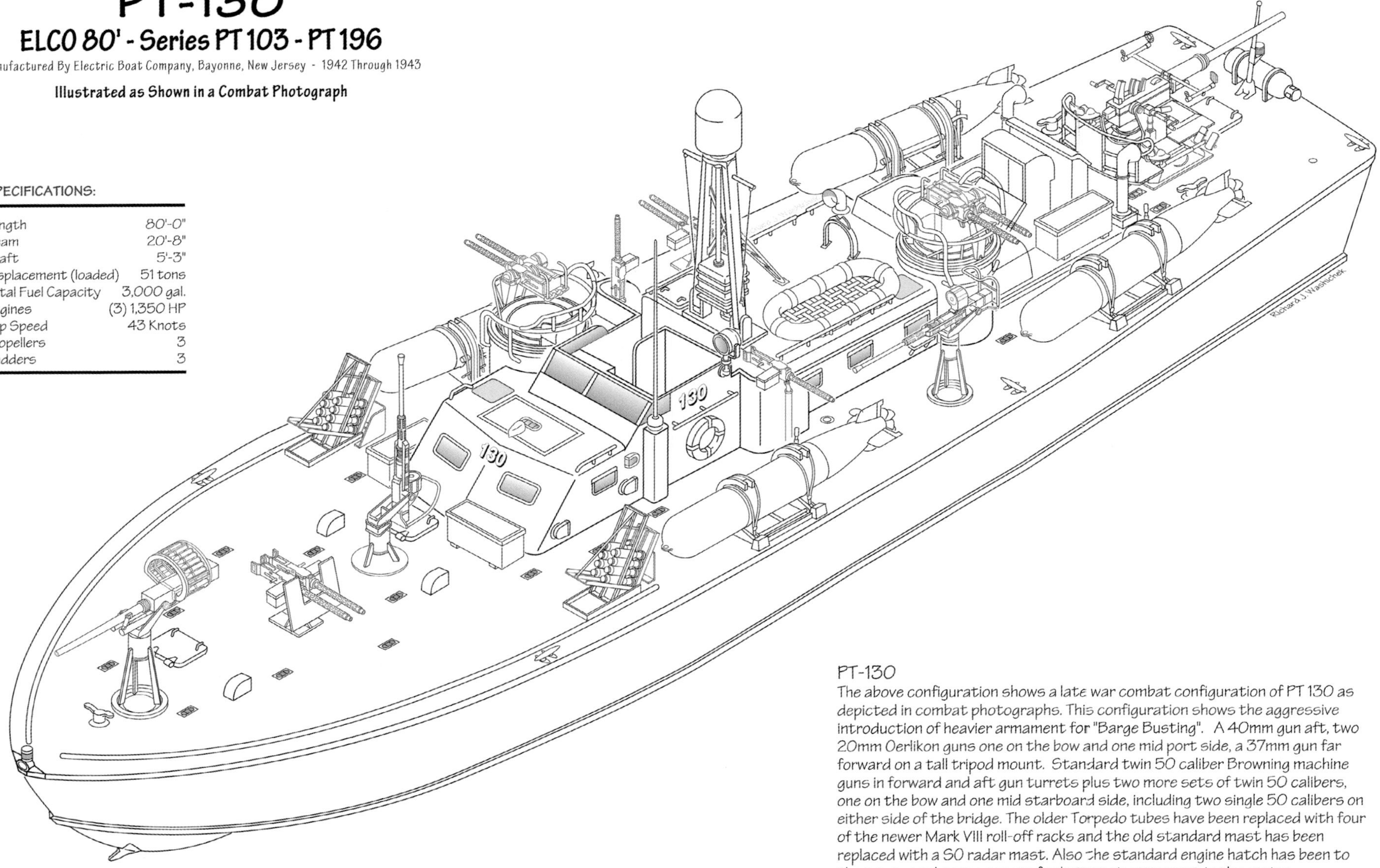

PT-130

The above configuration shows a late war combat configuration of PT 130 as depicted in combat photographs. This configuration shows the aggressive introduction of heavier armament for "Barge Busting". A 40mm gun aft, two 20mm Oerlikon guns one on the bow and one mid port side, a 37mm gun far forward on a tall tripod mount. Standard twin 50 caliber Browning machine guns in forward and aft gun turrets plus two more sets of twin 50 calibers, one on the bow and one mid starboard side, including two single 50 calibers on either side of the bridge. The older Torpedo tubes have been replaced with four of the newer Mark VIII roll-off racks and the old standard mast has been replaced with a SO radar mast. Also the standard engine hatch has been to the newer cowl scope access for better air movement in the engine compartment.

NOTE:

Placed into Service: Sept. 7, 1942 - Stationed in the Pacific with MTB Squadrons: Ron 7. Transferred to Ron 8 on Feb. 15, 1945

PT Boat Nickname: Raven

Illustrated & Copyrighted © 2007, by Richard J. Washichek

Courtesy of Richard J. Washichek

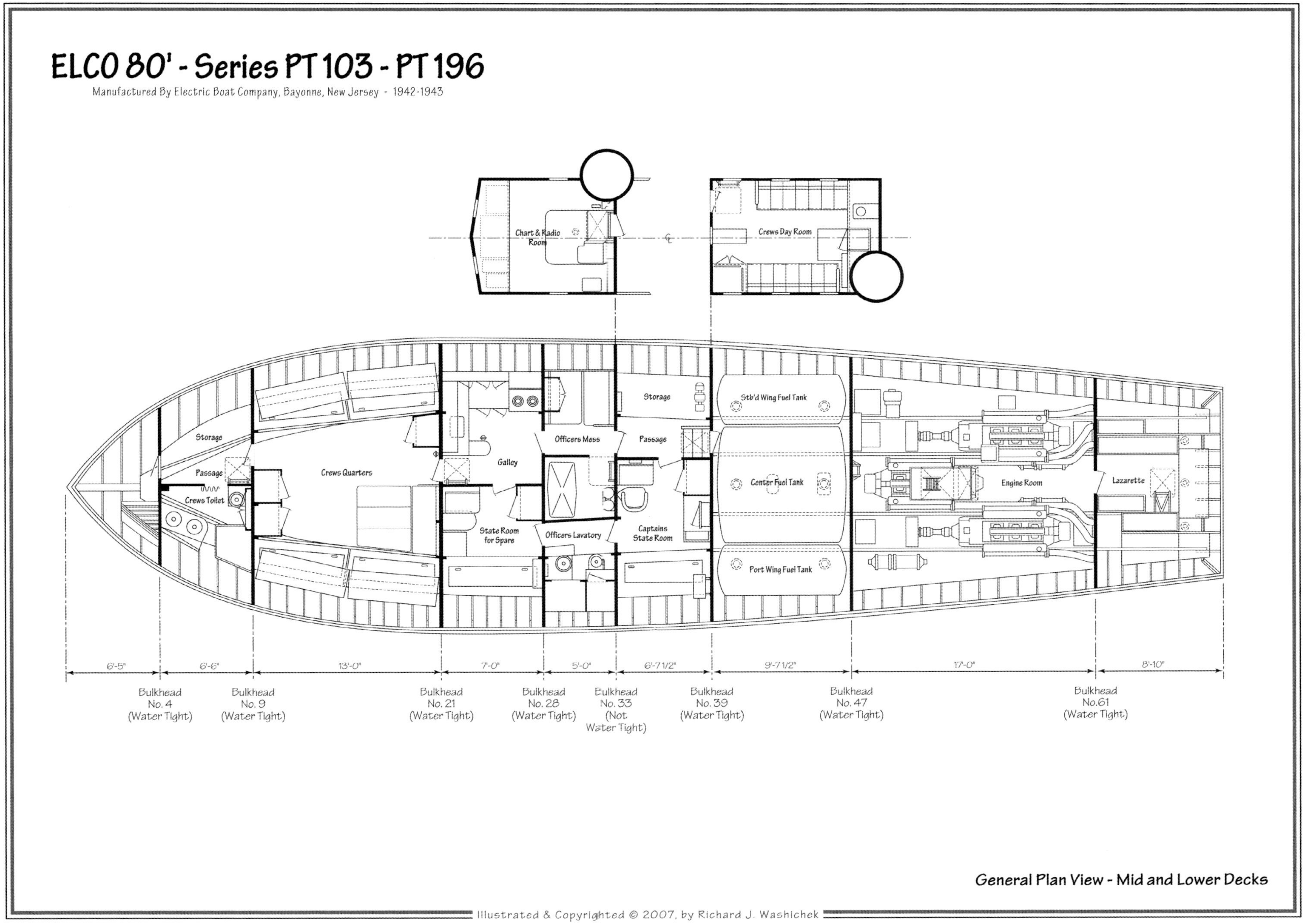

Courtesy of Richard J. Washichek

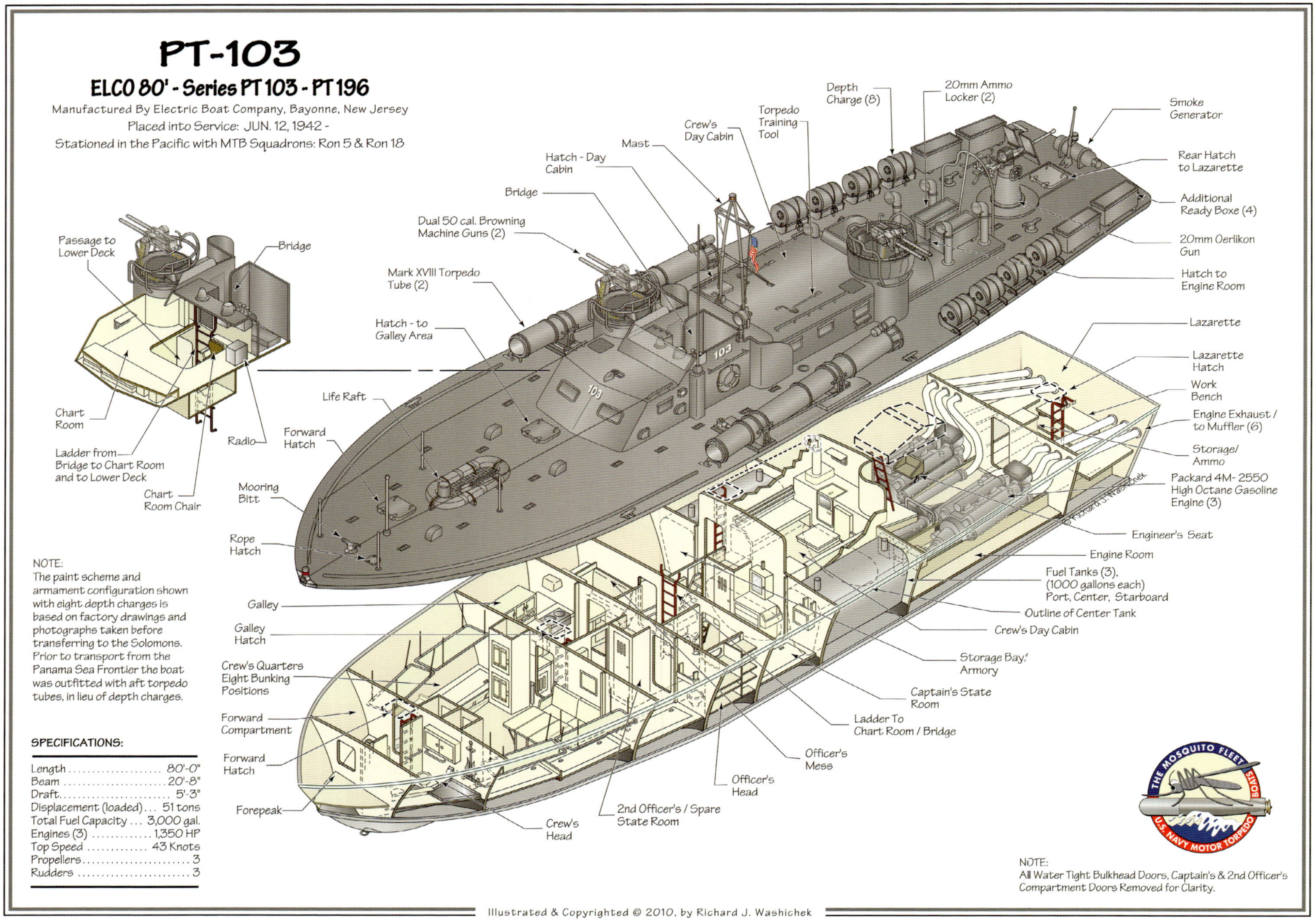

Courtesy of Richard J. Washichek

21

Tenders

PT boats, especially in the Pacific, could not operate without specialized care and maintenance by Tenders. The three converted yachts were not quite suitable. In 1943, nine converted LSTs were converted and commissioned with space for ships and equipment to lift the PT boat out of water. In 1944, better tenders were commissioned with specialized shops and a boom capable of lifting a PT boat on the forecastle. In all, 20 tenders (AGP-1 to 20) were commissioned. They took on the crews and the boats, handled refueling, and were used as a communication center.

AGP-1 *Niagara*, built as a yacht, was reclassified January 13, 1941, as the first tender. On May 23, 1943, a Japanese bomber made a direct hit on her forecastle and she went down with no deaths or serious injuries. *Courtesy of Frank Andruss*

AGP-3 Ron's PT37 and an unknown 77' Elco tied up alongside the USS *Jamestown*. *Courtesy of Ted Walther*

The AGP-3 *Jamestown* was built as a yacht in 1928 and reclassified as an AGP-3 on January 1943. It served as an escort for supply convoys between New Hebrides and Tulagi. Decommissioned on March 6, 1946, and sold, this boat was sunk near Panama in 1961.

AGP-5 *Varuna*, built as an LST and commissioned on August 31, 1943. It served at Palau, Marianas, Manila Bay, and Corregidor. It was sold in 1948.

This is an AGP-6 in Oyster Bay. *Courtesy of the U. S. Navy*

AGP-7 *Mobjack* was laid down as a seaplane tender. It was reclassified AGP-7 on March 11, 1943, and commissioned on October 17, 1943. It arrived at Dreger Harbor on July 27, 1943. It was decommissioned on August 21, 1946, and then sold for scrap.

USS *Oyster Bay* with PT boats in December 1944. *Courtesy of the National Archives*

Another view of AGP-7 *Mobjack*. *Courtesy of the U. S. Navy*

AGP-8 *Wachapreague* was laid down as a seaplane tender and commissioned on May 17, 1944. It saw action during the Battle of Surigao Strait. It was decommissioned on June 5, 1946.

AGP-9 *Willoughby* was laid down as a seaplane tender and commissioned on June 18, 1944. When it arrived in Mios Woendi it was credited with downing two Japanese planes in San Pedro Bay. On June 26, 1946, it was transferred to the US Coast Guard and sold for scrap in 1975. *Courtesy of the US Navy*

AGP-12 *Acontius*, commissioned June 1944. Its boom can lift a boat out of water and set it on the forecastle. It was decommissioned on March 22, 1946, and later scrapped.

AGP-6 *Oyster Bay* was laid down as a seaplane tender on April 17, 1942. It was reclassified as AGP-6 on May 1, 1943. It served in the Admiralty Islands, Pityili Island, and Leyte. It was decommissioned on March 26, 1957, and transferred to the Italian government on October 23, 1957.

AGP-15

AGP-18 *Chiron*, a former LST reclassified on August 14, 1944. After the war ended, it was decommissioned on April 2, 1946, and transferred to the Maritime Commission on November 26, 1947.

22

Restored PT Boat

PT658 Restoration

PT658 was scheduled to serve in Squadron 45, assigned to the Pacific. However, it was later scheduled for Lend-Lease transfer to the USSR. Due to the end of WWII, PT658 escaped the transfer and was sent to Port Hueneme, CA. In 1958 she was sold as surplus to a private owner.

A group of PT boat vets formed the Save the PT Boat, Inc., and took the relic into their custody. By the fall of 1994 the group had moved her to Portland, OR. From there the restoration took form. Volunteers labored to repair the boat and the three original Packard V-12 engines. Their aim was to restore the boat to its original Higgins design.

In June 2004 the boat was towed to Tomahawk Island Moorage. Since then, the boat has undergone continued restoration and daily maintenance.

PT658 is a prime example of the rare PT 625 class of Higgins PT boat. Higgins built 199 PT boats. Of the PT 625 class, there are only two hulls still known to exist in their original form: PT658 (Portland, OR) and PT796 (Fall River, MA). That PT 658 exists today is a miracle. It has been a daunting task to preserve and restore the boat because they were made out of wood.

Having the PT658 floating in water with operating original engines makes her the best example of all PT boats in the United States and the world.

This organization is nonprofit and needs and seeks public support (www.savetheptboat.com). PT658 is the only running PT boat in true WWII configuration in this country.

The crew renders a hand salute as PT 658 glides past USS *Shoup* (CG86). PT 658 provided an escort for the ship to start the Portland Rose Festival's Fleet Week. *Courtesy of Jerry Gilmartin*

PT 658 underway at 33.5 knots on the Columbia River during an Antique Classic Wooden Boat show on July 22, 2006. The boat has guns manned by PT boat WWII Veterans and a modern day crew. *Courtesy of Jerry Gilmartin*

23

Elco Plant Fire

There were two major fires that destroyed the old Elco and Electro Dynamic sites. The first fire was in 1963 and the second fire was on September 3, 2001.

Elco Division of Electric Boat Company, Bayonne, New Jersey

PT boats in various levels of assembly would be parked here during the War. Fire Chief Thomas Lynch would not let firefighters into the building for fear of a collapse.

The day after the fire shows the massive steel beam construction of Building 21. Water and debris cover the main assembly floor. *Courtesy of Frank Andruss*

The water tower with the Electro Dynamic logo was still standing after the fire. To the right of the tower is what was left of the boiler room. *Courtesy of Frank Andruss*

Appendix 1
List of PT Boats by Manufacturer

This list is courtesy of PT Boats, Inc. and compiled by Dick Washichek after countless hours of research and computer skills.

ELCO - Electric Boat Company, Bayonne, New Jersey

10-19	70' - Elco - Early development boats - Trans. to Britain	10
20-68	77' - Elco	49
103-196	80' - Elco	94
314-367	80' - Elco	54
372-383	80' - Elco	12
486-563	80' - Elco	78
565-622	80' - Elco - 22 boats never shipped out - War ended	58
623-624	80' - Elco - Contract canceled - War ended (2 boats)	0
731-760	80' - Elco - Kits to be assembled by Russia (30)	0
761-790	80' - Elco - Contract canceled - War ended (30 boats)	0
	Total Boats Built:	**345**

PTC's 1-12	70' - Elco PTC's - Trans.......... to Britain	12
	Total Boats Built:	**12**

HIGGINS - Higgins Industries, New Orleans, Louisiana

5-6	81' - Higgins - Development/Experimental	2
70	76' - Higgins - Reclassified as YP107	1
71-94	78' - Higgins	24
197-254	78' - Higgins	58
265-313	78' - Higgins	49
450-485	78' - Higgins	36
564	78' - Higgins	1
625-660	78' - Higgins	36
791-794	78' - Higgins	4
795-796	78' - Higgins - Reclassified as small boats	2
797-808	78' - Higgins - Contract canceled - War ended (12 boats)	0
	Total Boats Built:	**210**

HUCKINS - Huckins Yacht Works, Jacksonville, Florida

69	72' - Huckins - Development/Experimental	1
95-102	78' - Huckins	8
255-264	78' - Huckins	10
	Total Boats Built:	**18**

Canadian Power Boat Company, Canada

368-371	70' - Scott-Paine Design	4
	Total Boats Built:	**4**

Appendix 2
List of PT Boats Ordered by U.S. Government

This list is courtesy of PT Boats, Inc. and compiled by Dick Washichek after countless hours of research and computer skills.

Boat No.	Length / Manufacturer
Development & Experimental Boats	
1-2	58' - Miami Shipbuilding Co. -Reclassified. Small boat
3-4	58' - Fisher Body Works
5-6	81' - Higgins Industries (Sparkman & Stephens design) #6 sent to Finland
6	81' - Higgins Industries (new #6 after previous was send out)
7-8	81' - Philadelphia Navy Yard
9	70' - British Power Boat Co. (Scott-Paine design)
10-19	70' - Elco (Electric Boat Company) - Transferred to Britain
Production PT Boats	
20-48	77' - Elco
49-58	77' - Elco - Built as British BPT's 1-10
59-68	77' - Elco
69	72' - Huckins - Reclassified as YP106 a Patrol Vessel
70	76' - Higgins - Reclassified as YP107 a Patrol Vessel
71-84	78' - Higgins
85-87	78' - Higgins - Transferred to Russia
88	78' - Higgins - Transferred to Britain
89	78' - Higgins - Transferred to Russia
90-94	78' - Higgins - Transferred to Britain
95-102	78' - Huckins
103-196	80' - Elco
197	78' - Higgins - Transferred to Russia
198	78' - Higgins - Transferred to Britain
199-254	78' - Higgins
255-264	78' - Huckins
265-276	78' - Higgins - Transferred to Russia
277-288	78' - Higgins
289-294	78' - Higgins - Transferred to Russia
295-313	78' - Higgins
314-361	80' - Elco
362-367	80' - Elco Kit - Assembled by Harbor Boat Building Co.
368-371	70' - Scott-Paine - Canadian Power Boat Co. - (Scott-Paine design)
372-383	80' - Elco
384-399	70' - Vosper - built by R. Jacob Co. - transferred for Britain
400-429	70' - Vosper - built by Annapolis Yacht Works - Tans. to Russia
430-449	70' - Vosper - built by Herreshoff - Transferred to Russia
450-485	78' - Higgins
486-563	80' - Elco
564	78' - Higgins (Hellcat)
565-600	80' - Elco
601-622	80' - Elco - Never shipped to Pacific - War ended
623-624	80' - Elco - Construction stop, contract canceled - end of war
625-633	78' - Higgins - Transferred to Russia
634-656	78' - Higgins - Transferred to Russia
657-660	78' - Higgins - Never shipped to Russia - War ended
661-692	70' - Vosper - built by Annapolis Yacht Works - Tans. to Russia
693-730	70' - Vosper - built by Annapolis Yacht Works - Never shipped to Russia
731-760	80' - Elco - Transferred to Russia (Knock-down Kits)
761-790	80' - Elco - Construction contract canceled - War ended
791-794	78' - Higgins - Stricken form Navy Register
795-796	78' - Higgins - Reclassified as small boat
797-802	78' - Higgins - Construction contract canceled - War ended
803-808	78' - Higgins - Construction contract canceled - War ended

Appendix 3
PT Boats Placed in U.S. Navy Service

This list is courtesy of PT Boats, Inc. and compiled by Dick Washichek after countless hours of research and computer skills.

PT Boats Commissioned

Boat No.	Manufacturer	QTY
9	70' - Scott-Paine - Built by British Power Boat Comp	1
20-48	77' - Elco	29
59-68	77' - Elco	10
71-84	78' - Higgins	14
95-102	78' - Huckins	8
103-196	80' - Elco	94
199-254	78' - Higgins	55
255-264	78' - Huckins10	
277-288	78' - Higgins12	
295-313	78' - Higgins	19
314-361	80' - Elco48	
362-367	80' - Elco Kit - Assembled by Harbor Boat Building Co. 5	
368-371	70' - Scott-Paine - Built by Canadian Power Boat Co. 4	
372-383	80' - Elco	12
450-485	78' - Higgins	36
486-563	80' - Elco	78
564	78' - Higgins (Hellcat	1
565-600	80' - Elco	36
601-622	80' - Elco	22

PT Boats in Service Totals

Boat Type	QTY
70' - Scott-Paine Design Boats	5
77' - Elco Design Boats	39
78' - Huckins Design Boat	18
78' - Higgins Design Boats	138
80' - Elco Design Boats	296
Total in squadron service :	**495**

Appendix 4
PT Boats Not Placed in U.S. Navy Service

This list is courtesy of PT Boats, Inc. and compiled by Dick Washichek after countless hours of research and computer skills.

Ordered as PT Boats

1-2	58' - Miami Shipbuilding Co, - Reclassified small boat	2
6	81' - Higgins (Sparkman/Stephens design) to Finland	1
49-58	77' - Elco - built as British BPT's	10
69	72' - Huckins - Experimental - reclassified as YP106	1
70	76' - Higgins - Experimental - reclassified as YP107	1
85-87, 89	78' - Higgins - Built as Russian RPT's - sent to U.S.S.R	4
88, 90-94	78' - Higgins - Built as Russian RPT's - sent to Britain	6
197	78' - Higgins - Built as Russian RPT's - sent to U.S.S.R.	1
198	78' - Higgins - Built as Russian RPT's - sent to Britain	1
265-276	78' - Higgins - Transferred to U.S.S.R	11
289-294	78' - Higgins - Transferred to U.S.S.R.	6
384-399	70' - Vosper - Transferred to Britain	16
400-449	70' - Vosper - Transferred to U.S.S.R.	50
623-624	80' - Elco - Construction Halted	2
625-633	78' - Higgins - Transferred to U.S.S.R.	9
634-656	78' - Higgins - Transferred to U.S.S.R.	23
657-660	78' - Higgins - Built for U.S.S.R. but not shipped	4
661-730	70' - Vosper - Transferred to U.S.S.R.	70
731-760	80' - Elco - Transferred to U.S.S.R.	30
761-790	80' - Elco - Contract cancelled	30
791-794	78' - Higgins - Stricken from Navy Register	4
795-796	78' - Higgins - Reclassified small boat	2
797-808	78' - Higgins - Contract cancelled	12

Ordered as BPT Boats

21-52	70' - Vosper - Transferred to Britain	32
53-60	70' - Vosper - Transferred to U.S.S.R.	8
61-68	70' - Vosper - Transferred to Britain	8

Appendix 5
PT Boat War Time Losses

Legend:
A = Destroyed as a result of accident
D = Destroyed to prevent capture or Friendly-Fire
E = Destroyed as a direct result of enemy action

A	PT 22	Damaged in storm/Scrapped	01-12-1943
A	PT 28	Wrecked in storm	01-12-1943
D	PT 31	Grounded in enemy waters/Destroyed to prevent capture	01-19-1942
D	PT 32	Destroyed to prevent capture	03-13-1942
D	PT 33	Grounded in enemy waters/Destroyed to prevent capture	12-26-1941
E	PT 34	Destroyed by enemy aircraft (Strafing)	04-09-1942
D	PT 35	Destroyed to prevent capture	04-12-1942
E	PT 37	Destroyed by enemy warship	02-01-1943
D	PT 41	Destroyed to prevent capture	04-15-1942
E	PT 43	Damaged by enemy warship/Destroyed to prevent capture	01-11-1943
E	PT 44	Destroyed by enemy warship	12-12-1942
A	PT 63	Destroyed by fire in port	06-18-1944
A	PT 67	Destroyed by fire in port	04-17-1943
D	PT 68	Grounded in enemy waters/Destroyed to prevent capture	10-01-1943
D	PT 73	Grounded in enemy waters/Destroyed to prevent capture	01-15-1945
D	PT 77	Destroyed by Friendly-Fire U.S. Warship	02-01-1945
D	PT 79	Destroyed by Friendly-Fire U.S. Warship	02-01-1945
A	PT 107	Destroyed by fire in port	06-18-1944
E	PT 109	Destroyed when rammed by enemy warship	08-02-1943
A	PT 110	Lost in collision	02-26-1944
E	PT 111	Destroyed by enemy warship	02-01-1943
E	PT 112	Destroyed by enemy warship	01-11-1943
D	PT 113	Destroyed as a result of grounding	08-08-1943
E	PT 117	Destroyed by enemy aircraft (Bombing)	08-01-1943
D	PT 118	Grounded in enemy waters/Destroyed to prevent capture	09-07-1943
D	PT 119	Destroyed by fire in port	03-17-1943
D	PT 121	Destroyed by Friendly-Fire Australian aircraft	03-27-1944
E	PT 123	Destroyed by enemy aircraft (Bombing)	02-01-1943
E	PT 133	Destroyed by enemy shore batteries	07-15-1944
D	PT 135	Grounded in enemy waters/Destroyed to prevent capture	04-12-1944
D	PT 136	Grounded in enemy waters/Destroyed to prevent capture	09-17-1943
D	PT 145	Grounded in enemy waters/Destroyed to prevent capture	02-04-1944
D	PT 147	Grounded in enemy waters/Destroyed to prevent capture	11-20-1943
D	PT 153	Grounded in enemy waters/Destroyed to prevent capture	07-04-1943
D	PT 158	Grounded in enemy waters/Destroyed to prevent capture	07-05-1943
E	PT 164	Destroyed by enemy aircraft (Bombing)	08-01-1943
A	PT 165	Lost in transit, tanker torpedoed	05-24-1943
D	PT 166	Destroyed by Friendly-Fire U.S. aircraft	07-20-1943
D	PT 172	Grounded in enemy waters/Destroyed to prevent capture	09-07-1943
D	PT 173	Lost in transit, tanker torpedoed	05-24-1943
D	PT 193	Grounded in enemy waters/Destroyed to prevent capture	06-25-1944
A	PT 200	Lost after collision	02-22-1944
E	PT 202	Destroyed by enemy mine	08-16-1944
E	PT 218	Destroyed by enemy mine	08-16-1944
A	PT 219	Damaged in storm and scrapped	09-14-1943
A	PT 239	Destroyed by fire in port	12-14-1943
E	PT 247	Destroyed by enemy shore batteries	05-05-1943
E	PT 251	Destroyed by enemy shore batteries	02-26-1944
A	PT 279	Lost in collision	02-12-1944
E	PT 283	Destroyed by enemy shore batteries or Friendly-Fire	03-19-1944
E	PT 300	Destroyed by enemy aircraft (suicide attack)	12-18-1944
A	PT 301	Damaged by explosion in port and scrapped	11-07-1944
E	PT 311	Destroyed by enemy mine	11-18-1944
E	PT 320	Destroyed by enemy aircraft (bombing)	11-05-1944
D	PT 321	Grounded in enemy waters/Destroyed to prevent capture	11-11-1944
D	PT 322	Grounded in enemy waters/Destroyed to prevent capture	11-24-1943
E	PT 323	Destroyed by enemy aircraft (suicide attack)	12-10-1944
E	PT 337	Destroyed by enemy shore batteries	03-07-1944
D	PT 338	Grounded and destroyed not in enemy water	01-31-1945
D	PT 339	Grounded in enemy waters/Destroyed to prevent capture	05-27-1944
D	PT 346	Destroyed by Friendly-Fire U.S. aircraft	04-29-1944
D	PT 347	Destroyed by Friendly-Fire U.S. aircraft	04-29-1944
D	PT 353	Destroyed by Friendly-Fire Australian aircraft	03-27-1944
E	PT 363	Destroyed by enemy shore batteries	11-25-1944
D	PT 368	Grounded in enemy waters/Destroyed to prevent capture	10-11-1944
D	PT 371	Grounded in enemy waters/Destroyed to prevent capture	09-19-1944
E	PT 493	Destroyed by enemy warship	10-25-1944
D	PT 509	Destroyed by ramming enemy warship	08-09-1944
E	PT 555	Destroyed by enemy mine	09-08-1944

Summary of loses

A	Destroyed as a result of accident	12
D	Destroyed due to damage and to prevent capture or Friendly-Fire	33
E	Destroyed as a direct result of enemy action	24
	Total: **96**	

Appendix 6
Killed in Action

Adelman, Ens. William, I.
Adler, Donald, S1c
Albert, Raymond, S1c
Albright, Elmer, F., MoMM2c
Amos, Joseph G., RM3c
Andrews, Harry E., GM3c
Archibald, Robert J., S1c
Ausley, William, S., GM3c
Avant, Edwin H., MoMM1c
Badger, Lt. (jg) Samuel E., Jr.
Bales, Ens. Bruce S.
Ball, John W., QM2c
Ballough, Rudolph, MM1c
Banfield, Jerome C., S1c
Bangert, Ralph W., RdM3c
Barry, Joseph M., RdM2c
Bartell, Frederick O., GM1c
Basso, Albert J., S1c
Batchelor, Clifford, GM2c
Beaulieu, Richard J., S1c
Beauregard, Valmore W., F1c
Becket, Arnold F., TM2c
Beer, George J., MoMM1c
Bell, Jack O., SC2c
Bendl, Lewis J., S2c
Beneke, Ens. James R.,
Bennett, James G., QM3c
Berra, Vincent A., QM3c
Betz, Herbert H., QM2c
Blair, Donald F., S2c
Blaszkowski, Adolph M., WT3c
Boone, Albert E., GM3c
Bougere, Louis C., MoMM2c
Bowers, John R., MoMM2c
Bradish, Carroll E., EM2c
Breen, Daniel R., RM3c
Brendlinger, Ralph E., MM1c
Bricker, Darrel A., RdM3c
Brightman, William C., Machinist
Brine, William E., S1c
Brown, James T., CTM
Brown, John J., CGM
Brumm, Boyd W., GM3c
Brun, Ronald J., TM3c
Brunner, Joseph M., MM1c
Bucar Joseph S., MoMM2c
Burke, Lt. (jg) James R.
Burns, Frank N., MM3c
Campbell, John L., F1c
Canterbury, Morgan J., TM2c
Carpenter, Robert A., RM2c
Carpenter, William B., GM3c
Cary, Lt. (jg) DeWayne E.
Chalker, Joseph C., MM2c
Chester, Ens. John D.
Christiansen, Charles W., MoMM2c
Ciluffo, Domenic J., MoMM1c
Clayton, Alonzo L., RM2c
Cleary, Cornehlius C., Y1c
Coatsworth, John T., F1c
Cook, Ens. Frank E.,
Cook, William E., MM1c
Cookman, Lt. George E.
Cooper, Marcus W., MoMM1c
Cortese, Angelo R., GM3c
Cottom, Kenneth E., GM2c
Cowles, Donald H., MoMM1c
Cread, Walter I., F2c
Creelman, Lt. (jg) Brenton W.
Crist, Lt. Harry M.
Crowe, Willard A., QM1c
Curran, William J., Y2c
Curtin, Lt. (jg) Edward D.
Curtis, Robert H., RM2c
Cuthriell, Norman F., Jr., F1c
Dabakis, James J., TM2c
Daley, Lt. (jg) John F.
Daley, Willaim Jr., MoMM1c
Davison, James H., S1c
Dean, William R., QM3c
DeLong, Lt. Edward G.
Devaney, Thomas F., SC3c
Dhonau, Harvey H., QM2c
Donnell, Ens. John G.,
Duckworth, Ens. John C., Jr.
Dudas, William L., MoMM2c
Dunleavy, John J., GM2c
Dunner, John H., Cox
Eichelberger, Paul E., MM1c
Emmons, George D., Jr., GM2c
Ennis, Charles E., Jr., RM3c
Eno, William E., EM1c
Farnese, Joseph M., F1c
Ferchen, Richard H., RM2c
Fischer, Raymond B., CCM
Fiume, Samuel F., SC3c
Foley, Raeburn J., S1c
Foster, Albert P., S2c
Francesca, Albert P., SC2c
Fravel, Marcus L., F1c
Freeland, Lt. Frank
Fried, Jay V., GM3c
Friedman, David L., QM3c
Fries, Robert W., MM3c
Frudenfeld, Monte N., S1c
Fucili, Evo A., MoMM3c
Gaffney, William E., Jr., PhM2c
Gallo, Anthony F., S1c
Ganz, Edward W., SC2c
Giaccani, Floyd R., Bkr2c
Giddens, Roy A., MM1c
Gleason, Lawrence M., MoMM2c
Goolsby, Montie W., Jr., F1c
Gormley, John J., S1c
Gray, Elmer M., F1c
Greenhalge, William J., S2c
Gregory, Allen B., Jr., QM2c
Griebel, Lt (jg) Russell J.
Griffith, Glen G., CMoMM
Grizzard, Herbert N., MM1c

Gross, Philip S., QM2c
Guest, Harold R., TM2c
Harris, David W., TM2c
Hartz, George D., TM2c
Harvey, Malcolm L., SF1c
Haughian, Lt. (jg) Michael A.
Hawkins, Benton F., MoMM2c
Hayes, Charles R., Electrician
Haywood, Ens. Alfred W., Jr.
Heaton Ben A., Jr., MoMM2c
Hill, Warren J., TM3c
Hirsch, Willard E., S1c
Hix, Lt. (jg) Sidney D.
Hogan, Lt. (jg) George W. M. Jr.
Holland, Patrick, TM2c
Holloway, Earnest T., S1c
Hooper, Elvin E., GM3c
Horan, Charles E., S2c
Hornbrook, Ens. Philip R., Jr.
Horsfield, Richard E., MoMM2c
Hubbard, Lewis B., MoMM1c
Humrich, Clark L., MM3c
Hyde, Ens. Robert W.
Jackson, Clifford D., MoMM2c
Janusz, Stanley J., GM3c
Johnson, Herbert W., S2c
Jolley, Cerell C., MoMM2c
Juneau, Raymond T., S1c
Kaasinen, Wilho A., RM2c
Keefe, Joseph F., TM3c
Kelly, Ens. James J.
Kent, Ens. William H.,
Kiene, Charles B., F1c
King, Lloyd O., S1c
Kirk, George E., SF2c
Kirksey, Andrew J., TM2c
Klann, Ralph F., MoMM2c
Klesh, Joseph E., MoMM1c
Koerner, Woodrow H., MoMM2c
Kornak, Charles A., GM3c
Kossman, Lawrence C., S1c
Koury, Sam R., RM1c
Krenzar, Albin J., S1c
Kyriss, Jack, S1c
Laker, Andrew V., SC3c
Lampi, William A., S1c
Lane, Lt. (jg) J. Franklin, Jr.
Lee, Ens. Nixon, Jr.
Leeds Harry R., SC3c
Lengling, Raymond R., S2c
Leonard, Loyd W., S1c
Light, James D., CTM
Lindberg, Ray F., MoMM2c
Lindsay, Willard G., S1c
Line, Kenneth R., SC2c
Lossin, Marvin W., MoMM2c
McCarley, Turner E., MM1c
McCormack, Charles T., S2c
McDonald, James J., S2c
McKinney, Russell H., Jr., F1c
McKinney, William J., S2c
McLaughlin, Lt. (jg) Joseph D.
McMullan, John L., SC2c
Malone, William V., MoMM2c
Manley, Vernon A., GM3c
Narney, Harold W., MoMM2c
Marsh, Robert E., MM1c
Masters, John J., Jr., CMoMM
Mathes, Lt. (jg) James M., Jr.
Mercer, Lawrence D., MoMM2c
Midgett, Charles F., Jr., MoMM3c
Mills, Robert W., SC2c
Mitchell, Lt. Frank K., Jr.
Moore, Walter A., RM1c
Moorman, Ens. Madison K.
Morrone, Ugo A., S2c
Munoz, Louis L., S2c
Murray, Ens. Bond
Murray, Lt. (jg.) Howard L.
Muse, Clyde J., GM3c
Mysliwiec, John L., GM2c
Nanney, Robert M., CQM
Owsianny, Walter, MM2c
Pace, Robert J., S1c
Pacel, Joseph P., MoMM2c
Paris, Manley L., F1c
Pasterik, Ens. Ladislav T,
Paul, Bertis I., MoMM1c
Pavlis, Lt. (jg) John K.
Petrulavage, George, S1c
Pierson, Ernest E., BM2c
Pinkley, Ens. Clarence L.
Plant, Ens. William H.
Posey, William H., SC1c
Przybys, Richard, MoMM3c
Rakowski, Edward A., RM3c
Ramsdell, Arthur C., TM3c
Rauch, Robert W., MoMM2c
Rayl, Norman H., SC2c
Raymond, Lt. Jonathan S., Jr.
Regan, Richard A., Machinist
Reilly, Raymond R., TM2c
Reynolds, Tony S., RM2c
Reynolds, Willard J., CCStd
Ricci, Alfred A., GM3c
Rice, Glen C., S1c
Riedl, John J., SC3c
Rihn, Burnell V., TM1c
Robison, Clark L., S1c
Rodgers, Ernest E., Jr., RM1c
Romeos, Raymond A., BM2c
Ross, Thomas M., GM1c
Rothenberg, Leigh, Jr., TM3c
Rouleau, Raymond A., MoMM2c
Sabello, Cyril A., S1c
Saganiec, Stanely A., SC2c
Saliba, George, SC3c
Sammartino, Vito A., F1c
Saul, Lt. (jg) Robert M.
Saul, William K., SC2c
Schaffroth, Rudolph W., TM2c
Scharmuck, David A., GM3c
Schmidt, Edgar L., TM2c
Schwerdt, Arthur J., QM1c
Scranton, Leroy W., Jr., MM3c
Senese, Alfred O., S1c
Shaffer, Lt. (jg) Paul F.
Shaw, James J., Jr., MoMM2c
Sherman, Ens. Rex A.
Shribman, Lt. (jg) Philip A.
Sileo, Leonard, MoMM2c
Sippin, Victor, MoMM2c
Smith, Edward, Boatswain
Smith, John C., Jr., S1c
Sorenson, Milton C., GM3c
Sparrow, Norman R., MoMM1c
Spaseff, Paul P., RM2c
Speer, William J., TM2c

Spicher, Paul L., RM3c
Stadler, Lt. (jg) Herbert
Stambaugh, William A., CY
Stanley, James D., M3c
Staples, Ens. Parker W.
Stearns, Floyd M., CEM
Stillman, Lt. John H.
Stockwell, Donald L., S1c
Stone, Allen R., Cox.
Stuckey, Vesper D., Sr., StM1c
Sutherland, George D., MoMM2c
Sutton, John T., QM3c
Tatarek, Anthony P., SC1c
Taylor, Lt. (jg) Cyrus R.
Taylor, William W., SK3c
Thale, Edward C., QM2c
Thomas, Dewey C., MoMM1c
Thompson, Ferree E., Jr., S1c
Thompson, John, S1c
Tigner, Gerald R., MoMM2c
Todd, Merwin K., GM2c
Trevisano, Cosmo, GM2c
Turnbull, William C., Jr., SK3c
Vining, Thomas R., Jr., RM3c
Wachsmuth, Jack H., Jr., M2c
Wackler, Russell J., RM2c
Wajert, Frank J., S1c
Walker, Lt. (jg) Daniel T.
Walker, Frank C., GM1c
Walkington Keith L., S1c
Wallace, Joseph T., TM3c
Walters, Leonard F., F1c
Walters, William N., S1c
Walzhauer, Allen F., GM3c
Watson, Warren R., F1c
Webb, George T., MoMM1c
Weber, Nevil T., Jr., MoMM3c
Wicks, Leslie W., S1c
Widstrand, Roy P., F1c
Wilkerson, William R., MoMM2c
Willett, Charles A., MM3c
Williams, Thomas C., Jr., SK2c
Wingfield, Richard H., S2c
Wisniewski, Stanely, QM3c
Wypick, Walter P., GM3c
Yensan, Robert E., SF3c
Youngs, William H., QM3c
Ziethen, Ens. Freddrick A.

The tumult and the shouting dies-
The captains and the kings depart-
Still stands thine ancient sacrifice
An humble and contrite heart.
Lord God of hosts, be with us yet,
Lest we forget - Lest we forget!

Kipling

This beautiful stone was created by artist Mr. Robert Voorhees under the direction of Frank J. Andruss, Sr. Andruss is the owner of The Mosquito Fleet Exhibit, which is a traveling display of hundreds of PT boat related artifacts. Funds for this stone were generated by PT boat veterans and local businesses. It was unveiled to invited guests at a ceremony on May 31, 2004, Memorial Day. The stone is part of the Memorial walkway at the Massachusetts Veterans Memorial Cemetery, located in Agawam, Massachusetts.